MW00928136

God's Perfect Plan

My Story, My Testimony, My Life

Vergie Iglus

Vergie Iglus

God's Perfect Plan

My Story, My Testimony, My Life

Copyright 2019 Vergie Iglus

ISBN: 9798642314234

All rights reserved. No part of this book may be reproduced or transmitted in any form or by any means, electronic or mechanical, including photo-copying, recording, or by any storage or retrieval systems without the written permission of the author except in the case of brief quotations embodied in critical articles or book reviews. The persons in this book and their stories reflect people living and deceased, some of the names have been changed to protect their privacy.

Auto Biography/Christian/Gospel Music

Scriptures taken from the original King James Version of the Bible, and English Standard Version, 2001 by Crossway. New King James Version 1973,1978,1984 by International Bible Society.

This book was printed in the United States by Kindle Direct Publishing. Available on Amazon.com and other fine retail book outlets.

Acknowledgments

I would like to thank God, my Heavenly Father for providing the material for this book by allowing me to live the experiences that I have written in it. Surely He had a "perfect plan" for it all.

As one of the lines in the song title states , " How could I know, this was the better way?" **Job 23:10**- He knows the way I have taken when I am tested, I shall come forth as gold.

Many thanks to my Editor , Linda Meaux, who suffered through my ignorance of how it all should be done. Thanks for your patience your understanding and endurance. I couldn't have gotten through it without you. Yes! He had a "perfect plan " that Saturday at the Sweet Dough Pie Festival, when you heard me singing " *The Blood",* and you dropped everything and ran over to the flatbed where I was singing. Surely He had a perfect plan to send me someone of like faith to assist me with such precious cargo. Thank you for seeing it to the end.

To my Pastor Derald Weber who has been more than a pastor to me, but a friend and confidant who has supported me and has been an anchor in my life. He has shown so much genuine love to a precious little soul that God placed in my care.

And for sweet, First Lady, Karen Weber who has also been right there in my corner, encouraging me, edging me on at my low points. She included a part of my story in her publication stating that it had the potential to reach, and help many hurting people. So, after laying it aside for some years I knew I had to finish the book.

I also would like to give thanks to Marlon Adair, Stephenie Haney Montes, Anastasia Riddle and Karen Weber for their participation on my last CD, "Higher Heights."

I must express my many thanks to my good friends Rhonda and Terry Jennings for being the best friends ever, for faithfully picking me up, and making sure I got to church whenever I didn't have a ride, and have been my support in so many other ways. They have truly been a blessing in my life. I call them not only friends but my Sister and Brother.

And to Tiffany Robicheaux of KAJN radio for upon hearing my music, and reading my bio, suggested and prayed unto God that He would somehow allow me to write a book about my life. She predicted that the lives of many hurting people would be touched.

For He knows the way I have taken, when I am tested, I shall come forth as gold. **Job 23:10**.

Dedication

To my beloved son William that will remain forever in my heart. Also, to my two grandbabies Terrance Andrews and Julian Laday who were with me during my struggles.

Preface

Some may call what I have written in this book, "airing my dirty laundry, but I believe God has directed me to write this book. There are many more who have suffered much more than I have suffered, and hit bottom and feel there is no way up. But there is a way, Jesus says, " I am the Way, the Truth and the Life." **John 14:6 KJV**

There are some who will never realize this truth, unless we tell our story. God has a reason and a purpose for everything that happens in our lives. I am so glad He gave me the wisdom to go to my son William 'that day' and tell him I was divorcing him. It made all the difference in the world. I am so glad I didn't shun him because of what people would think. I was not ashamed of him. I loved him with all my heart. His struggles were my struggles. His battles were my battles, and they all belonged to God.

God loves us with an everlasting love, and He expects us, whom He has called by His name, to love others unconditionally, without respect of person.

I have seen children of families from all walks of life, from good homes, Christian homes, rich homes, poor homes. Single parents and both parents struggle with neglect and abandonment. We need to throw out the lifeline to those who are perishing. Those who are sinking in despair. We are the hands, the feet, and the mouth of Jesus. We need to occupy until he comes.

PART ONE

CHAPTER 1

Life on the tobacco farm

My name is Vergie Hines Iglus and I was born in Calvary, Georgia, in Grady County to Willie Gus and Rebecca "Beck" Hines. But I was reared in Attapulgus, an Indian name meaning dogwood, eight miles away in Decatur, County. Our family worked on a farm that grew tobacco. We harvested those crops for the Morgan Family, Mr. Warren and his sons, Bubba, Marvin and Philip.

Between the tobacco seasons the fields were used to grow vegetables. We had our individual gardens. We grew all kinds of vegetables just imagine it and we grew it! Including some this generation never heard of. And we ate everything we grew in our garden from collard greens, cabbages, turnips, mustard greens, string beans, okra, field peas, crowder peas, sweet, potatoes, red potatoes, watermelons and corn.

The corn that was grown for the farm would be ground up into corn meal and sold to the workers. There was an abundance of fruit trees and in season as the fruit ripened we canned and preserved it in glass Mason Jars.

We even "shook" peanuts. Most of this generation today don't have a clue where peanuts come from. We pulled them out of the ground when they were ripe, shook the dirt off, washed them and boiled them while green. In their dried state we roasted them in the hot ashes in the fireplace.

Sugar Cane was also grown in season from which syrup was made. "We would drink some of the juice before it was cooked down into syrup. It was delicious!"

Some families that lived on the farm raised and butchered hogs and made good use of every part of the meat. Most families on the farm like my own family raised chickens. "I will never forget wringing the neck of a chicken that had been shut up to fatten them up for cooking. This was also the method of consumption for cleansing. The chickens were then dunked into a pot of boiling water, to loosen the feathers, so they could be pulled off easily. Even though each family raised their own chickens, there was also a chicken farm in my hometown. I can remember seeing the long wired cages full of all white chickens. Now it's hard to imagine chickens being cage raised that long ago."

I began singing in church when I was twelve years old, at the Baptist church in Calvary, Georgia, in 1947. While in school my music teacher selected me, a shy little girl, to sing with a trio. I didn't realize until that time that God had blessed me with a special gift of singing .

I was a Mama's girl I wanted to please her in every way. I sat by the fireplace with my head on her lap until she was ready to go to bed, then I would go to bed. I was always one to put others first, even as a child. I was protective of my Mom. I didn't want to burden her with my trivial needs or desires. I would hide from her the fact that I had a stomachache or was hurting in any way, because I didn't want her to worry.

There was the time when she could only afford to buy Easter dresses for my two older sisters, Earvie, and Pecola. She apologized to me for not being able to buy one for me. Oh! That was just fine. I understood. That is what I said to her, when in fact, I was deeply disappointed. But I didn't want my mother to worry.

My Dad worked in the woods, as some men did in those days, sawing down trees for wood. My mom would prepare lunch and send it to him at lunchtime.

One day when she was about to send Monkey to bring him his lunch, I asked permission to go with her. Well previously I had injured my knee. It had become infected, but I didn't make a fuss about it. I didn't want to worry my mom. She told me I couldn't go into the woods with my bad knee. " you can hardly walk" she said. "Yes, I can" I said, "I'll walk like this." I demonstrated for her, my bad knee drawn up in pain, I went limping along for her. But I didn't go to the woods that day.

11

My dad was a hardworking, man, dedicated to his family. I have never know a more hard working man. All his life he was well known, and well loved by everyone. But, he would literally, physically fight for his family if he had to. He also had a drinking problem. He would get drunk and physically abuse my mom.

My mom would sit out in the wood pile in the yard when this happened. I would sit in the wood pile with her. This was the place where the wood was kept and cut up to be burnt in the fireplace, to keep us warm in winter.

We would sit there until daylight would peep through, and we would walk the short-cut (through the woods) to my mom's sister, Aunt Rosie. This was from Attapulgus to Amsterdam, about three miles. Then when my dad sobered up, he would come and get us and bring us home until the next time it happened.

I loved my dad, but I resented him for how he treated my mom. However, I have many fond memories of him. My brother Billy and I hardly have a phone conversation without falling out laughing over some quote of my Dad's or something he did. He passed away at age ninety- five.

Three Lifechanging Events

At age fourteen I got "religion." Every year we would have a preacher come for a five day revival. We sinners would sit on the mourners bench. I had been told by the older women. "Honey, when you get religion it don't cut off your pleasure." In other word it meant, you just keep on doing what you were doing, sinning.

Thursday night came and I hadn't felt a thing. I had not been able to shed one tear. I was determined I would not let the preacher leave, without me getting religion or I would have to wait a whole nother year before I got it.

So, on Friday night as he whooped and hollered and periodically spit tobacco juice into a tin can filled with sand I squeezed my eyes and a few tears came out. When he was finished he went up and down in front of the mourners bench extending his hand to the mourners.

"I took his hand and that meant I got religion. The following Sunday those of us who had 'got religion,' were baptized in the Flint River."

Also, I was just fourteen when I began working in the tobacco fields. The processing of tobacco was done in many stages from start to finish. It went from the field to the barn where it would be prepared and sorted. Out of this process came cigarettes, cigars, chewing tobacco and snuff.

While working in the barn and packing house, the women would sing church songs. I was always asked to lead the singing even though I was the youngest one in the building.

Folks would tell me that I had a 'pretty voice'. I would lead the singing and there seemed to be a domino effect. The melodious sound would spread all over the building. This was the most beautiful sound I had ever heard. The harmony was perfect. I could imagine this was how the Angels sounded in Heaven. I looked forward to a long day's work, just so we could sing.

That same year my mother got sick. We didn't have hardly any knowledge about medical diagnosis in those days. It got to where she couldn't lie down to sleep. She would sit up in her rocking chair, and I would sit up with her.

We had no electricity back then. My mom would get hot and I would sit there fanning her with a cardboard fan. I would give her medicine when it was due.

My mom became worse and the local doctor ordered her to be taken to the hospital in Tallahassee, Florida, for further treatment. I can't remember how long it was that she stayed in the hospital. But my dad would take turns bringing one of my sisters, or brothers to visit with her.

It was my turn to go visit Mom next, and I was so looking forward to it. I remember the day I got the news of her death. I was going house to house selling packages of gardening seeds. I was devastated that I never got my turn to see her, and more so that she had gone and left me at all. My mom was only thirty-nine years old when she passed.

At the age of seventeen my older sister Earvie Mae, had gone to Brooklyn, New York, to live with my mother's brother, Uncle Johnny. As Mom grew worse she would grieve for her asking for her constantly.

She wanted to see her badly. Her grief may have contributed to her illness.

But it was too late! Mom passed away before she made it home. Earvie Mae' decided not to return to New York, but stayed to do what she could to help with the younger ones.

There were two younger sisters Betty and Remell. I was seven years older than Betty and babysat for her for mom while she worked in the tobacco barn. So, I kind of thought of her as my own child.

After my mom's death, my dad's sister Rosie Lee asked for her and she went to live with her in Quincy, Florida. Now I was grieving the death of my mom, and the loss of my little sister. I couldn't wait for the rare visits to my Aunt Rosie Lee to get to see my little sister Betty. My parents had two children prior to the birth of Earvie Mae. I was told they were beautiful babies with curly black hair, but they did not live long after birth.

According to an old wives tales someone told my Mom when they had another child to nickname it after an animal. The next child born was a girl. Thus, she became known as 'Monkey.'

My Dad soon moved on with his life and he moved a woman named Rose, whom he had previously known, into the house. Unknown to us my dad was giving Miss Rose his salary, and also that of my sisters and brothers. She was sending the money to Camilla, Georgia, to have a house built for them.

Vergie Iglus

On the day Earvie Mae found out about this she had a disagreement with Miss Rose and then she moved out of the house. She moved in with Mrs. Roxann and Mr. Henry who lived on the farm, just down the road. Willie Butler also lived with them, he was Mr. Henry's stepson and also my boyfriend that I was for sure going to marry. He was the tallest, handsomest man I had ever seen. We would marry but we were not going to live on the farm.

Willie had asked me to marry him, but we had decided to wait until I had finish high school. He had finished school the year before me. I was in love and couldn't wait for school to end so we could be married.

On weekends Monkey, Willie and I would go down the road to the town part of Attapulgus, which we called 'Hack'. We would get something to eat from the 'hole in the wall'. Then we would do a little shopping, and head for the Juke joint. Willie and my sister would go inside to dance the night away. I wanted to live "right" like my mother. So I avoided the 'sinful' things like going inside a juke joint. I would stand outside and wait and wait.

Once when it seemed, they were going to stay all night, I became frustrated and decided **to wa**lk home. I had to pass the graveyard to go home and I was scared to death. There were no such thing as streetlights, and it was pitch dark so, when I got near the graveyard I took off like a jet.

My dad and some of the older men on the farm loved to tell

scary tales to us which we loved to hear. But after hearing them we were scared to go to bed. One such tale was of two dead men who would argue over the person that they saw passing in front of the cemetery. To settle the argument, they would break a stick and if you looked back it proved to them who was right.

When the house was finished in Camilla, Rose moved out with the intention that my Dad would follow her. On Saturday my dad loaded the pickup truck for the move to Camilla. But before Dad could leave town the Morgan's sent a man to falsely accuse him of owing $800 dollars to him.

They didn't dare approach my Dad themselves. The man asked the new boss from Camilla that had hired him if he was going to pay the debt. But the man was not willing to pay that much money, which was a fortune in the day. So, my Dad quickly unloaded the truck. The following Saturday my dad and my younger brother Buddy took the bus and they left the Morgan Farm. No! they couldn't outsmart my Dad. He was a modern day Jacob.

At age 17, I broke down and allowed Willie Butler to teach me to dance. Singing had been my first love. And I sang to to the tunes of Johnnie Ace and Sam Cook, before his gospel career) and Fats Domino. They were my favorite artists. Now dancing had become my second love.

Vergie Iglus

Willie and his stepfather were not getting along at that point and his mother thought it best that they be separated. She sent him away to her sister in Miami, Florida. We maintained a long distance relationship for a while, but slowly we drifted apart.

He moved on with his life in Miami and I started dating a 'uniform'. That's what I was impressed with, not the soldier that was wearing it. Because I was still in love with Willie.

I was very independent at an early age. I continued going to school and got a job at a Methodist Parsonage, cooking for a pastor and his family. I went to Sunday School and attended church every Sunday. I made the honor roll each year in high school ,which is when they would start honor roll back then.

My teachers had recommended that I skip a grade and move to a higher grade but I wasn't as smart as they thought. I was dumb! because I would not go. I was a shy little girl in a sense. I don't know to this day why I wouldn't move up except I wanted to stay in the classroom with my older sister, Pecola.

I could feel a longing for God way back then. There was this void in my heart for something more than I had.

One day I was walking to work, at the parsonage, I picked up a tract, a brief religious pamphlet, I read it. It must have been a reading for Sunday school kids. I was fifteen, or sixteen. That was the most precious piece of literature I had ever read. I read it and I cried and cried. I memorized it and I remember a good bit of it until this day.

This is what I remember. *"One day Saul was sick . He could not eat anything. He could not drink anything. Saul was blind . He could not see. He could not see the green grass. He could not see the blue sky.* Then God led Saul to Ananias… and it went on to tell of Saul's conversion. God was dealing with me, and I didn't know it. I kept that little reading in my heart, and it would comfort me.

By now I felt trapped on the farm and determined that I would have a better life. I had plans for my future. I went to Sunday School and Church and worked my way through high school. I had determined at any early age not to marry a man from a farm, but a man who worked in an office and wore suits, so I would not have

to patch 'overalls', (men's britches.)"

But God had other plans for my life… *Jeremiah 29:11, For I know the plans I have for you, declares the Lord, plans to prosper you and not to harm you, plans to give you hope and a future. Romans 8:28 says, "And we know that all things work together for good to those who love God, to those who are the called according to his purpose. (NIV).*

He confirmed this in a song he inspired me to write later on.

"God's Perfect Plan."

I made preparations for my future.

I would fill it with great richest and fame.

I would be on the list of the who's is who.

And men would know my name.

I would travel the whole world over.

I would see all the sights made by man.

I thought in my heart I had it all worked out.

But God had a perfect plan.

My life took a turn in a new direction

Down a path, that I did not foresee

how could I know this was the better way,

and that God had designed it just for me.

But God had another plan.

Chorus : *He is the potter, And I am the clay,*

I am yielded in his hand.

I wouldn't have the victory in my life today,

except God had the perfect plan.

Yeah, Yeah, he had the perfect plan.

On this path there were stumbling blocks on the road,

And this way I didn't understand.

But He stayed right there

And through it all. He never let go of my hand.

He led me through the streets of hard trials,

And to places unfamiliar and strange.

You see, he was molding me,

and making me and preparing me.

So, my whole life He had to rearrange.

For you see,

He is the potter and I am the clay,

I wouldn't have no hope,

No how, no way.

Vergie Iglus

Except God had another plan.

Yeah, Yeah, Yeah,

He had the perfect plan.

PART TWO

CHAPTER TWO

Farm life Trials

When we worked in the tobacco field we got paid by the day. We worked from sunup to sundown. But when we worked in the barn we were paid by 'piecework', meaning the number of tobacco sticks we would fill up on a string and tied to sticks that were about four and a half feet long to be hung in the barn to cure.

One day when we were working in the barn stringing tobacco I was accused of cheating. Some of the other women were known to cheat by not putting enough leaves on the sticks, to use them up faster to get paid more money.

On another day Neil, the straw boss, was counting the leaves on my stick and falsely accused me of cheating because he knew Philip Morgan, the big boss, was listening. And before he could finish counting Philip growled at me, "You have been cheating all day."

I replied, "No, I haven't."

He repeated , "Yes you have."

I was still standing behind the table and replied, "I haven't."

Then he jumped at the opportunity to chew me out , "Get out!."

I replied , " I will ."

Then because I stood up to him he said, "You stink." Meaning I needed to change my attitude. And I replied to him, "You stink!"

Then I climbed over the sill behind the table and headed for the door. I heard him running behind me . He was a big and tall man that wore about a size 12 to 14 boot. I just knew he was gonna kick me. As I looked back I stumbled and caught myself on my two hands. I quickly jumped up and he was right up on my back. I reached up and nailed him right under the eye with my fist.

I shouldn't have taken pleasure out of that, but he was going to kick a shy, little14 year old girl, with his size 12 or 14 boot. I already had resentment in my heart for the opposite race, but this incident only increased it. I was cautious knowing what would happen when black folks would cross the Morgan's. And I was determined that very day I would leave the farm.

I ran home to pack and was going to take the bus to Camilla to my dad's. My sister, 'Monkey," had just had a baby and asked me if I would walk to the store and get her some milk. After I returned with the milk I was going to take the bus to Camilla. My sister told me Phillip, the man I had the altercation with, had come by her house inquiring of me.

He told my sister he didn't know what had gotten into me. He had only praise for my work, said I was his best worker and asked that I return to work so he could make amends.

Philip also told Monkey, "I told my wife that Virgie and J.D., arc the only two that go to Sunday School." He never had any reason to mention this until now.

At that time neither J.D., nor I knew the real truth. When I was born again years later I realized there was much more truth and light to walk in. The apostle Paul tells us as Christians we are children of light. The apostle Paul made this statement in **2 Cor.3: 2 Ye are our epistle written in our hearts, known and read of all men.**

Phillip was reading our lives when he was riding up and down that dirt road and watched J.D. and I faithfully go to church each Sunday. The lost are not interested in what we say, they are reading our lives.

What Philip had told my sister surprised me as I knew what they were capable of doing. Two days later I went back to work, and Phillip would look at me out of the corner of his eyes as if trying to figure me out.

The Morgan's were known for treating their hired hands harshly, (mostly the men). I would watch them kick these men. I would wonder, Why would the men allow themselves be treated like this. I thought they are men, too.

But they had liberty to go and come, and do whatever, as long as they didn't take their families and move, at their will. I knew families who would try to get away at night, but to no avail.

Because all of the "goods" that were secured during the year, the syrup, corn meal, meat, and borrowed money, made them indebted to the owners and legally they couldn't leave. They would find them and bring them back. My dad was one that stood up for himself and his family and he was very well respected. I can hear him clearing his throat as he started off, "Looka here white folks…" My dad had quiet the life story before he moved us to the Morgan Farm.

Even though the Morgan's own wives did not work, there was always a woman in each of the bosses homes, their jobs were to cook and clean and babysit. Everyone who went to the bosses homes had to enter through the back door even though we worked there

As a little girl I played with Mason Morgan's oldest daughter Beth. Then when I grew older, I became his cook and baby sitter. One summer, the family went to Apalachicola, Florida, for their summer vacation. They took me along to cook and take care of their two girls. I got to enjoy the beach and the water. I would get in the water with the kids, but I couldn't swim, so I used an inner tube .
So, it was not all bad, all the time.

The Iglus Family Arrived on the Farm

Vergie Iglus

A family from Alabama had just moved to the farm, with a name that no one had ever heard of "IGLUS." One that I have never been able to figure out especially how I ended up with it!! There was a story behind the name It was supposed to have been changed from Brown to Iglus. Supposedly they were fleeing some kind of disputes over land that was owned by the Iglus.'

The husband and the wife were complete alcoholics. They worked from sunup to sundown, like the rest of us, Monday thru Friday, but from Friday, at the end of the workday, to Sunday afternoon, they didn't know who they were. I have never seen anyone so totally "drunk."

And they were hoarders. You couldn't find a space in the house they lived in to walk, much less sit down. And it was all clothes ,on the walls, on the furniture, and on the floor.

There was plenty of moonshine going around on the farm , and they consumed more than they share. They had five boys, and one girl who was born with Down Syndrome Disorder. Up until 1965 children with this disorder were called Mongoloid's because of their facial features. She was the only girl born in the family until.my oldest son Walter got married, and they broke the cycle. Their second child was a girl. Then their son had a girl .

Well, one of the boys started stalking me, his name was Walter. I was not interested in him in the least. I had friends, boys that I would go out with on weekends. They were mostly dancing partners. Dancing

28

had become my hobby. None of us drank, and drugs were unknown to us in those days. We just had fun dancing to records played on a jukebox.

My sister Earvie, stayed home a lot those days because she now had a baby to take care of. Walter started hanging out with her around the house. And each time a friend would bring me home he would be there waiting.

I detested coming home finding him there knowing he was stalking me. One day I was sitting on the wash bench on the side of the house. He was there talking to Monkey who was sitting in a chair. He had a BB gun in his hand and for no reason at all aimed it at the wall right above my head.

He would go to the store and buy me ice cream, candy, anything he thought I wanted. I would often order things from mail order catalogs and he would go to the post office, pay for them and pick them up for me.

Before I knew what was happened I planning to marry Walter. Surely God had another plan. One day my brother Billy and some other boys were playing checkers and overstayed their lunch break. Mr. Marvin went to get them and reprimanded them harshly. My brother having my Dad's spirit, was not having none of it

Billy went home and told my sister he was leaving and going to Camilla. I was not about to let my brother leave me. We were inseparable. We did everything together, we played together, and the mischievous things we did cant' be numbered. We would do them and fall all over each other, on the ground laughing about it.

We do the same thing today by phone reminiscing about those long past times, he residing in Georgia and me in Louisiana.

In the meantime, Walter's brother, Willie James, met my brother on the way to the bus and decided, "I'm coming with you." And he did!

The next day Walter , myself and a friend took off for Camilla. Walter and I were planning to get married at the courthouse in Camilla, but we didn't get the chance We all went to Camilla to spend the night at my Dad and Miss Rose's. We were going to look for us a place to live.

When we knew anything, the Sheriff was knocking on Dad's door. Warren Morgan had sent them to pick us up and bring us back to the farm. My Dad told us not to worry that he would have his boss Mr. Cox get us out the next morning. It just showed how much my dad cared for us. But we were transferred to the Bainbridge jail the next morning.

Warren Morgan had sent my Uncle Lee with a proposition for us. We could either be good little "Hired Hands " or we could stay in jail until we learned our lesson.

We all agreed to go back to the farm. I felt so hopeless at this point, and really felt trapped. When we got back to the farm Warren Morgan looked at us and said, "Can't let y'all go. Don't yah know, y'all's some of my best workers."

I didn't know God in the way that I needed to know him, and wondered sometimes, where was He.

Married life Begins

Walter and I were married in the courthouse in Bainbridge. I don't know if what I heard was really true. Walter told me much later that he and my sister's husband 'PJ', Paul went to Madam Ace a card reader, to get her to put a spell on us to make me us marry them.

I did not have the Holy Ghost at that time so there is a possibility that it did work. I was only nineteen and married when my "Storms" began. I knew God had a plan for my life. But was this His plan or the plan of Satan. But if there is any truth in the power of darkness working in the life of an unbeliever, then it worked on me.

My husband Walter gambled, drank, and was very abusive, because of unfounded jealousy. He had jealously demons. We were men and women, working together in the barns and fields. We would go home for lunch, depending on where we were working he watched me like a hawk.

When we would get home, he would say" "I saw your man looking at you." If I denied it, I was lying, if I kept quiet, I was ignoring him. Either way, I got a lick upside my head. I did not know God but somehow I knew that there were certain morals and principals to be followed from what my mother had taught me, from a child and I had learned obedience.

I thought that in a marriage you shared everything with your spouse I guess I was super ignorant. So, when this very handsome guy, T.J, made this statement to me, "You mean to tell me you married somebody like HAPPY JACK's son? With the shape you have, you coulda married someone like Jackie Robinson." Walter's dad's name was Ralph, and his mom's name was Moselle.

Believe me, I was not trying to make him jealous when I repeated this to him. I honestly believed I was doing what a wife should be doing. I was determine to be faithful to my marriage and make it work. In spite of my husband's jealous outrages and physical and verbal abuse. I remained in the marriage, leaving him for brief periods of time then going back for the sake of the boys.

We had three boys and I did not want them to grow up without their father. Once, when I left him and went to my sister's house, he took the baby, and brought him to his mom. He promised to bring him back when I came back home There was only one choice for me at this point. My baby was my life. So, I went back to face more abuse. He didn't care where we were, if this evil spirit came over him he would beat me, and kick me, even in the street.

Shortly after my first baby was born, I went back to work. Suddenly my right eye became irritated. It seemed that in one day it became inflamed. The town doctor treated everything. We didn't know what a specialist was in those days. He treated the eyes, he was the dentist, he pulled out teeth with what appeared to be wire pliers, without deadening the nerves.

I remember going there with my sister Pecola to get her tooth pulled, and she would come out of the chair and go down to the floor, writhing in pain, screaming for dear life, and there was blood galore. We sure have come a long way since then.

Dr. Welch treated my eye the best he could and sent me home. The pupil of my eye was completely covered with a thick white skin. It was determined that it was an ulcer that originated from a grain of sand, while working in the field. Dr. Welch sent me to a specialist in Tallahassee Florida. to have it removed. It was a Father and Son team named Adams. I got to see the son, who burned the ulcer off with a laser, and sent me home to continue treatment with Doctor Welch.

My eye got progressively worse. I had to take care of the baby while Walter worked. And that became an impossible task. We moved back in with 'Monkey" so she could take care of the baby. I suffered excruciating pain day and night. It was slightly better during the day, but at night, I would cry out in pain. It seemed as if every tooth in my mouth was hurting. I later learned that it was the nerves in my mouth. My sister would make home brew from fermented corn. I would drink that to null the pain.

After going to Doctor Welch numerous times without any improvement , he told me my eye was full of infection, and needed to come out. Believe me when I tell you, I was more than ready for that eye to come out. So that same Philip Morgan that was ready to kick me offered me encouragement.

He told me that it was nothing to be ashamed of and he said they would give me a glass eye. And I wouldn't be able to tell the difference.

There was a lady, Mrs. Willie Gaines, living on the farm who was his cook, and the kids Nanny that had only one eye for as long as he knew her. But she did not get a glass eye it was just a socket right there and not a pleasant sight. Even glasses would have helped. I thanked him for his concern and encouragement , but I was ready to trade that pain for a glass eye as soon as I possibly could. My sister made the appointment and Walter drove me to Tallahassee, Florida.

I would like to interject here that none of us really knew God, but we would watch religious programs on TV. We knew of Oral Roberts and his healing ministry and my sister had written to him asking for prayers for me.

Well I eagerly told Dr Adams what Dr Welch had told me and was anxious for him to get on with the business of removing my eyeball. But he proceeded to examine my eye. He shined the light in my eye and repeatedly asked if I saw anything. I could see a shadow, like when your eyes are closed you can still tell that there is movement going on. But I repeatedly denied seeing anything I just wanted the eyeball out.

But he wouldn't give up. He kept shining the light, and waving his hand , finally I timidly admitted I could see a shadow. It seemed he was so relieved. And made his big announcement " I'm not about to remove an eyeball that still has sight in it" he said .

And you have to know that back in those days, that was God at work. He said he had researched my medical history and discovered I had birthed a baby. I had gone back to work too soon, and my immune system was low and was not responding to the medication.
He also gave me strong vitamins and some drops for me to use at home.

When Walter and I got home, my sister was in the front room watching the ball game, along with some friends. I fell across the bed, because it was the front "bedroom". She read me a letter she'd received from Oral Roberts informing her that by the time his letter reached her, "her sister" (me) I would be healed. I had not even known that she had written to him. I fell asleep and slept " hard" for the first time in a long time, because of the pain. I woke up and I was in for a big pleasant surprise . God had done a marvelous work on my eye.

There were big chunks of puss coming from my eye, and there was no pain. My eye was sore to touch, but no pain. I can give God all the glory, because it was He that used that kind and concerned Doctor Adams to persevere and not give up. But insisted that I admit that I saw something that made my eye worth saving. That was back in the days when people of color were not treated equal with the other race even when it came to medical attention .

Yes! once again, God had another plan. The only sign that I have is that that there is scar tissue somewhere on the eyeball, but I never loss my sight . Praise be to my awesome God.

After my eye was better, Walter, the baby and I moved back home. We shared one side of an apartment with another couple Quinester and Bobby. As I was rolling dough one day to make biscuits, my hands suddenly started swelling. They literally looked like toad frogs in minutes, and I felt excruciating pain. Quinester came over to assist with the baby and stay with me until Walter and Bobby got home.

The doctor's offices and clinics closed at sundown. But if there was an emergency a doctor would meet you at the clinic. The doctor only lived next door to the clinic. Walter called the doctor and we went to see him. He took a look at me , gave me aspirin. He told Walter to bring me back the next day for a full exam. I suffered in agony all night. The next morning Walter took me back to Bainbridge and I was diagnosed with rheumatic fever.

We had moved into the house behind Mason's when I became pregnant with William, my second son. And the abuse continued. By this time, he was not only drinking and gambling, he was giving our money to another woman, and staying out with her most of the night.

Lawrence, (Walter Jr.) and I would be left alone with no wood cut for the fireplace, to keep us warm. He was not yet two years old. A friend would come over and cut wood for us and bring it in for the fire. When Walter finally got home and found out the friend had brought wood, there was more abuse.

One day I heard a noise above my head . I looked up and there was this big snake crawling on the rafters. We did not have ceilings like we do today. Goodness, I don't know how we ever made it. There was just the tin tops and boards covering the roof. We had wood stoves, wooden windows ,that swung open and we smoked the mosquitoes at night.

We bathed in wash tubs, because we didn't have plumbing, or running water. So, we had "out houses." When I saw the snake, I took my babies and a chair and sat outside until Walter got home from work. I was deathly afraid of snakes and I still am.

The abuse continued. Walter did not stay home. He was unfaithful and stayed out all night. I couldn't take any more. I took the two boys and went to Calvary. Mr. Howard Strickland had built a new house right across the yard from Aunt Rosie and Uncle Lee and I moved in with my babies. The cycle continued. There I was running to Aunt Rosie because of abuse just like my Mom. My Mom and Aunt Rosie had married two brothers, so we children were double first cousins.

At the end of the week Walter was there making promises to do better and begging me to take him back. I refused two or three times.

He would return each week with his promises. I finally broke down for the sake of the boys. I was always hoping that things would improve so that they could grow up with their father. I had always been a person to put others needs ahead of my own, even if I had to suffer.

Walter moved in and the abuse continued. He continued to gamble, drink, and chase women, one in particular. One day when I walked to the store I ran up on the two of them. She was sitting on a bench and he was standing with his arm around her My instinct kicked in like it did that day in the barn and I reacted in a not too positive manner, and I slapped her.

I had not yet heard whether there be any Holy Ghost. It was common for men and women to almost openly carry on an affair. You were considered popular to have a man on the side even if you were married. I thought it was disgusting. The preacher, the deacon, some of the married men and women on the farm all practiced this.

"Once before I was married, a married man who was already having an affair with one of the girls on the farm sent me a message requesting an affair. I sent a reply to him that I'm sure he didn't expect . I told him to go where the devil lives.

To my regret I told Walter of the incident. But it only helped to trigger his jealous rages. It was the same old accusations, "I saw your man looking at you ." I would deny it and get a lick. I would keep quiet and get a lick upside the head. I was either lying, or ignoring him.

One day when he drew a shotgun on me, for no reason at all, my Uncle Lee would have taken him out if Aunt Rosie hadn't stopped him.

Then I became pregnant with my youngest son Kendrick and again, it was like hell on earth. I went through the pregnancy by the hardest. The time came to deliver the baby. It was the Fourth of July. We had gone to a ball game in Reno, Georgia two miles away.

I was ready to leave before Walter got ready to leave. He was totally upset. In a fury he jumps in the car with me and the two kids, and takes off in a frenzy. It seemed it was just a matter of minutes before we would have a deadly crash. The more I pleaded for him to slow down the faster he went. We came to a corner where he had to at least slowed down. I opened the door and jumped out of the still moving car.

He stopped the car to gather me up. It was a foolish thing to do, but that was the only way to get him to slow down. It was half spite, and half just because I just didn't care anymore.

The next day was Sunday, the fifth of July, and I went into labor and I hid it. I was mad, I was hurt from the day before. Here I was getting ready to have a baby and I was no more thought of than a nuisance who wanted to leave the ball game too early.

Well I would show him! I would not let him know I was ready to have this baby. I was having labor pains when my cousin Carrie Lee came across the yard to my house. I didn't tell her anything, but she could see something was wrong.

She went and told her mom, and she knew what was happening My Aunt Rosie Lee informed Walter that I was in labor. This was the first baby I had planned to have in the hospital , because it was the first time I had taken out insurance

Kendrick was almost born before we got to the hospital. They had to call the doctor when we got there. They tried to make me wait, but the doctor got there just in the nick of time.

I managed to ask him what it was, half sedated he told me it was a boy. I slurred, " I wanted a girl."

He said. "Maybe the next one will be a girl."

I, slurred again, "There won't be a next one," and there never was.

We went home from the hospital and the abuse continued. By this time, I didn't care about anything anymore except my babies. I was beginning to believe it was not worth it being faithful, and loyal.

By this time my sister Betty had left Camilla to come to Amsterdam to stay with Aunt Rachel, my Dad's aunt. I went and got her to babysit Kendrick while I worked. It was clear that Walter was not going to change his ways. He threw his weight around always accusing, always, watching, always chewing on a cigar, always physically abusing me, gambling ,drinking, and chasing women.

Finally, I took my boys and went to my cousin Louise's house, and sent Betty to our older cousin's Sadie's house until a house that Mr. Howard was having built would be finished. When the house was finished we moved in. Walter followed me everywhere I went like a puppy dog. One night I answered a knock at the door, had I not slammed it shut in a split second, a butcher knife would have gone right through my heart.

It was him! He had seen a man talking to me in the fields and was jealous. I took out a peace warrant on him. He ran away to New Orleans to join his brother and find work.

A couple of months later, that same year he wrote and asked me to come to New Orleans he wanted to be a husband and " father. " I didn't want my children to grow up without their father, so after sending Betty to Monkeys.

I caught the bus to New Orleans. There was no Interstate back then, so we rode along the Gulf Coast. I was the only one awake the kids were asleep. I had never seen so much water in all my life. We were so close to the edge, I thought we could tumble over anytime, and we would all drown.

But we made it to New Orleans, safe and sound. We arrived on a Wednesday morning early. I didn't know what to think of the big City. All I had heard about it is when I relayed to someone that I was going there they stated that I was going to the City where all the witchcraft was. That morning, the streets were covered with trash, and debris. I learned later that it was the morning after Mardi Gras, whatever that was.

41

Walter had told me in his letter that he had secured housing for us, but that turned out to be another lie. He was shacking up with his brother Lamar and his wife, Mattie. And they were shacking up with her parents, Agnes and Jack.

The boys and I moved in with the crew Lawrence, (Walter Jr.) who was five, William three, and Kendrick one. We soon found a place to move into, and the abuse resumed. I had started a correspondence course in Nursing, because I didn't want to leave the boys with anyone, nor could I afford to pay anyone.

Walter would beat me, just because, and the boys would witness it all. Lawrence was traumatized by it. I didn't realize just how much this had affected him until one day we were walking home from church and he told me" Momma, when I get nine years old, I'm going to get a job, and take care of you." And added, when Daddy was beating you, I wanted to help you, but I was scared."

It broke my heart. He was always protective of me. That is why, when I was tarrying for the Holy Ghost, he fought those who were praying with me.

At this point, my story is becoming very sad, and my tears are beginning to flow.

I am so grateful to God that He saved me so, I could bring my boys to Him. When Lawrence got married, he got filled with the Holy Ghost. He broke that cycle. He never laid a hand on his wife. He has been the closest one of my boys to me. He got a job at age fourteen at city hall, through the school program and helped to support us. And he never stopped working until he retired

More about how he helped me later in the book!

Walter had a job, but not sufficient enough to support a family. Plus, he gambled and spent money on wine. I gave up my pursuit of a nursing career and got a job.

Agnes' mother, who was Walters brother's wife and I became friends. She lived a double life, which didn't seem to be much of a secret. She was half living with another man. Her husband Jack was an alcoholic, and so was their daughter Mattie. By now, I had come to believe that what Agnes, and many others that were shacking up was just a normal way of life. The abuse had taken its toll on me.

As I witness to everyone I can possible reach today, no matter what sin they are practicing I know that I don't dare judge or condemn. You can't do better until you know better. And someone has to tell them better. Lord let that someone be me.

I have not always done what was right in God's sight, and still do things that displeases Him. I have had to ask his forgiveness for some awful things and he forgave me. He has cast them into the sea of forgetfulness to remember them against me no more. I had become blind as a bat. The God of this world had blinded my mind as he has so many others.

43

As the apostle Paul says in **1 Corinthians 6:.11** *And some were such of you", but you were washed, but ye are sanctified, but ye ae justified in the name of the Lord Jesus Christ, and by the Spirit of God.*

Mattie died at an early age, leaving behind a husband a daughter and three sons.

The Milsaps' were the first family I met when I got to New Orleans. They became my friends, and more like my family. They invited me to a Baptist Church, that I "joined."

We went to church on Sunday mornings, and on Sunday night, we played cards, for fun, and drank beer. For some reason, they even gave my toddler baby Kendrick beer.

The thought had come to mind that, I was now in the big city, so I had to conform to it. Bernice and Jimmy Milsap had two children, Jimmy Jr., and Janice.

I got a job at the Sheraton Charles Hotel. At first I was working in the laundry then after just two months that job ran out. Since the laundry was closed on Sundays I was able to go to Church. I continued to play cards, and drink beer with Jimmy, Bernice and the other young couple, that were in our circle, Marcella, and Robert.

The more I went to church, the less fulfilled I became. I wanted more. Something was missing. There would be certain rituals that were carried out, like baptism, communion etc. During that time the lady ushers would dress in long sleeved uniforms and white bonnets and come rocking down the aisle singing.

The lead singer was tall and stocky and had a voice like a trumpet. After church I would find her in a situation where she would be using that same voice cussing like a sailor.

I was later to learn in the word of God that as true Children of God, these things ought not to be. In *Ephesians 4:29* Paul tells us, "Let no corrupt communication proceed out of your mouth, but that which is good to the use of edifying, that it may minister grace unto the hearers." ((KJV)

But before my eyes were opened I could not distinguish the difference. Another thing I observed was there was this one lady that would fall out every Sunday and go backward over the bench. They would take her out to the foyer and use smelling salt to bring her to. *Oh, how I wanted to feel the spirt that way.*

At that time, I perceived this was the the spirit of God. On Sunday nights she would have to be taken out of the bar room the same way, drunk. I didn't think nothing of it because I had been taught as long as you give God the first part of your day, you're good. That's all he requires."

A year later, Walter went to jail for six-months for non-child support. He never paid a dime. He said, "No white man gonna make me take care of my children."

Vergie Iglus

I worked my back to the ground, literally to take care of my three boys. I earned enough money to pay rent, and the babysitter. My kids were always hungry.

Times were really hard, and when he got out he resumed stalking my house and would parade in front of the house to see if any man would come in. During this time I reunited with him briefly but it wasn't going to work. He was spending money on other women and buying wine instead of feeding our children.

Finally, when my oldest son Lawrence was five years old, I couldn't take any more. I ended seven years of abuse "for good."

I was recalled to work at the Sheraton Charles Hotel, to work in the pantry and later worked as a vegetable cook. I was always singing my Sam Cooke, Johnnie Ace and Fats Domino songs, and I would mix in my "Church songs."

My co-workers would hear me singing and comment on my "beautiful" voice. One of them introduced me to a young lady, Iola Robertson ,who worked in the Hotel. She was a big fan of Mahalia Jackson and loved her songs. We had something in common, so we became friends.

Times were still very hard.

I could not make ends meet for my children. Then I met this man named Johnny at the Hotel and started going out with him. We would go dancing at the clubs and I started sipping highballs and beer. He would help me meet the financial needs of my children and myself. Being ignorant to the Word of God, and Satan the god of this world having blinded my eyes I went around testifying that "God had sent someone to help me take care of my children. I was telling everyone, "God sent me a man!" I was living the "good life."

Johnny and I would go out dancing and partying. He bought wine for my neighbor lady so she would watch the children. After a while I started getting sick and threw up the beer and Highballs.

One night after going out I was sleepy and probably tipsy from the alcohol I'd consumed. I went to bed with a lit cigarette in my hand and fell asleep. Then I was awakened and realizing the mattress had caught fire. I got up and poured water on it without waking the boys that were sleeping on a mattress on the floor.

Then something began to happen. God started to deal with me... I felt this void, this loneliness in my heart. Nothing satisfied anymore. A voice seemed to speak to my mind these words. " You are in this big city by yourself, and you're going to need somebody." I would come home, gather my boys and go inside and cry and cry; and I didn't know what I was crying about.

I began searching for what it was that I was missing. I even attended a rosary but left unsatisfied. The longing in me continued something/someone kept pulling me, drawing me. I know now that it was the Spirit of God.

47

I finally told Johnny I couldn't see him anymore. He was not going to take no for an answer. But every time he came looking for me and my boys were nowhere to be found.

We'd gone to church. I wanted to do something with my life. I had to work on Sunday's so I could only attend church on Wednesday nights.

The church had a midweek choir and I made a request to join. I was accepted but was told I had to have a robe in order to participate. There was a choir member who had an extra robe that she was selling for eight dollars. I didn't have eight dollars, so I couldn't buy it.

I was told by the choir director, "You have to have money to participate in things like this." I was crushed. There was an event coming up, and our midweek choir was on the program . As they sang, I sat there through the entire service and cried my heart out. It had nothing to do with the Holy Spirit, my heart was broken.

I just wanted to sing for the Lord. I look back now, and I thank God I did not fit in, He had a greater plan for my life *"A Perfect Plan"*.

When I had first joined the church; the head usher, a married man, made a pass at me. For the first time I did not find it flattering. I felt violated. I was searching for the way to serve God, and live right for Him. Surely this was not the place. The Spirit of God kept drawing me, this longing, this desire to fill that deep void within me.

My New Birth

Finally, I accepted my friend Iola Robinson's invitation to visit her home. She was new in the Lord and had never witnessed to me. We attended a fellowship in a little prayer room where services were being held until they found a building. There was something different about this small group of people, that numbered about seven dedicated folk. I felt loved, the love of God. I couldn't stay away after that.

The minister, Sister Banks, in her wisdom, would feed my children and me after everyone else went home. Then she would send the kids to play in the yard while her husband sat on the porch swing to watch them. She would take out her Bible and read to me and explain what she had read.

This was only about the second or third time that we had attended. It was when she read and explained from **Hebrews 13: 4 (KJV)**... Marriage is honorable in all. And the bed undefiled: but whoremongers and adulterers God will judge.

It was then I learned I was lost and on my way to Hell. I didn't say anything, but silently vowed that I was going to give my life to Christ.

The following Sunday service, when the altar call was made, I tried to go to the altar but found myself glued to my seat and couldn't. I was so disappointed that I couldn't do what I wanted to do. But I was not going to let Satan defeat me.

When I got home that Sunday I left my children in the apartment and went downstairs to the payphone to call Sister Banks. I was crying and

I told her that I was going to give my life to Christ.

She responded, "I know you are darling" I then told her , "I have this man in my life and he helps me with my children and if I let him go, my children will starve." Even though I had made up my mind that I was not going to see Johnny anymore, the devil had taken one more shot at me. He spoke to my mind and said, if you give your life to Christ, you will NEVER be able to enjoy the pleasure of sin anymore. For a moment, I was scared to death of what I wouldn't be able to do. Satan didn't expect me to tell her the truth, that would be exposing him.

Sister Banks said to me, "Darling, I'll put my head on the chopping block, if you let this man go, and give your life to Christ, God will provide for you and your children."

The next service I did it! I ran to the altar and repented of my sins. It seemed as if a ton fell from my body when I repented, and a fountain opened up inside of me. A barrel of tears flowed from my eyes, since then, nothing has ever been the same.

When the I went to the altar that Sunday and gave my life to the Lord, my life was changed forever. It is not a fairy tale, or a cliché that the light gets brighter and the trees get greener, it is real.

I had never read the bible story of Saul's conversion, but I experienced it just like in the book of **Acts 9:18** that said...And immediately there fell from his eyes as it had been scales and he received sight forthwith, and arose, and was baptized. I couldn't believe how much brighter the light had become. No one would ever be able to convince me that this born again experience was not the real, supernatural, divine, miraculous work of God.

Back in those days, we would kneel at a wooden bench in the front of the church, and tarry for the Holy Ghost. I tarried for a few times. But didn't pray through. There were two reasons for this, first of all, my oldest son, Walter/Lawrence, would fight those who were praying with me. He thought they were assaulting me just like his Dad used to do. The other reason was that I had Johnny on my mind. Not that it was difficult to give him up because I had done that when the Spirit of God began to draw me.

In those days when you were breaking up with a man it was usually because you had found another man. This was the last thing I wanted him to think. It seemed I had to detach from him. It was like I had to be free from one marriage to become married to another.

It had been a while since I had seen Johnny. We had no way of communicating, phones were rare, and we used pay phones. He would always just pop up; it wasn't like I had made plans to see him when he made deliveries at the hotel. Lately, he never found us at home. Next time Johnny would run into me, he would tell me he had been to my house looking for me and had missed me. I was so proud to inform him, "I was at Church. " Once he said to me, "If you ever leave me, I will kill you" well I was longing to see him to inform him that I was indeed leaving him. I had a holy boldness. I had no fear of him. I was covered with the blood of Jesus, and nothing or no one could harm me.

Sis Banks realized it was a task for me to pray through to the Holy Ghost with my son fighting and screaming, so she suggested that I come to the prayer room alone on that coming Saturday afternoon when I got off from work and leave the kids with my friend, Iola.

Well, we all know that God has perfect timing. Johnny and I hadn't run into each other in weeks. That Saturday I had just changed out of my uniform, and was ready to go take the bus, He came in with a delivery. I had to pick up my kids from the babysitter, take another bus to take them to Iola's. He saw that I was leaving and asked if I needed a ride. Just what I was waiting for.

After a short time in the truck, I announced to him that I couldn't see him anymore. He just calmly asked, "it's another man, huh?" And I couldn't have been more proud to announce to him, "There will never be another man, except the Man, Christ Jesus." I don't believe anything else much was said. We picked up the kids, dropped them to Iola's, and I headed next door to the prayer room

The Church had not yet been built Sis Banks, and Bro Banks got ready to tarry with me for the Holy Ghost. I was a shy, twenty-five year old single Mom, yes shy, especially in front of Bro and Sis Banks. So, you would have to know that it was a supernatural force that took hold of me that night.

No one can explain this glorious experience. Each and every one has to experience it for themselves. I was on my knees, so I just mopped up the floor. I received a double dose of the Holy Ghost. It seemed I spoke in tongues for hours.

What a life changing experience. I was so hungry for God and strove to do everything He required of me and more. Before I was saved I was flattered when men would comment on my outward appearance and my body. Now I despised their comments and the attention. I quickly changed the way I dressed. I wore longer, looser dresses to cover the shape of my body.

I told my friend Bernice about the church and the new life I had found. I could only visit them on occasion when I was not working or in church. They had taken my boys and me under their wing and we had formed a bond with them. But now when I would go to their home they would completely ignore me, as if I wasn't there.

I was crushed!

They would play cards and wouldn't say a word to me, but I stood my ground. I choose my life with God over their friendship.

It was no more than a month later that I had won Bernice and her family over, and they became a part of the family. After they became a part of the church we became very close again. They lived in Mid City and we lived in the 9th Ward. They would invite the boys and I home with them after church for lunch every Sunday.

Vergie Iglus

After receiving the Holy Ghost, and upon returning to work at the Hotel, I began sharing my testimony right away. No one had done anything to lead me to the Lord, but Satan was going to do everything he could to turn me around. No! He was not giving up on me that easy.

When I told John, the cook of my experience, he preceded to teach me a bible lesson. Among other things he told me, "There is no hell, you know. Hell is just a place where the Jews burn their garbage." By the time he finished, some kind of spirit had taken a whole of me. I was confused, and my head was spinning. I didn't know what had happened to me.

Once again, I managed to make it through the day. I made it home, and ran to Sis Banks with my woes, and once again she reassured me with the Word. The devil had made another attempt to get me to change my mind about my decision to serve God.

My boys and I lived in an upstairs apartment next door to a lady that was a Church goer, but she never saw the need to witness to me, in spite of my lifestyle. Of course, she believed what I was taught, way back when I was fourteen, and got "religion" in the Baptist church when I told her of my experience.

The lady further stated "Honey! God didn't call no Woman to preach" But she had come too late to inform me of that. I knew what I had received was neither of man nor woman. It was the supernatural, divine power of God, and no one could take it away from me.

I invited Marcella to church, and she came numerous times each time she cried, and cried, but she never gave in to the Spirit of **God**. She died at a very young age without knowing Him, leaving her husband Robert, and two children behind. Please read this scripture in **Hebrews 3:15** "While it is said, Today if ye will hear his voice, harden not your hearts, as in the provocation." **(KJV)**

Love Overflowing

I was on fire for God. I would witness and share my testimony to everyone who would listen. I would open my mouth and Words would flow out of my mouth and i had no control over what was coming out. His word was coming alive inside of me. Jesus had taken his abode inside of me, He was living inside of me, and he was speaking through me. This was so surreal. It was amazing! Jesus had said this would happen in **Matt.10:20,LUKE 12:12,Ex.4:12)**

Another thing that happened to my heart after receiving the Holy Ghost, is that it seemed that a purging took place immediately The resentment that had been built up all those years from what 1 had experienced from the white race just vanished. It was manifested when I returned to the Hotel.

Just as the light was brighter, and the trees were greener, my white co-workers looked different. I saw them through the eyes of love. My heart was filled with love for them. Thank God for what He was doing in me. All I could do was praise Him. I carried my Bible everywhere I went. I would read it on my break, and every Day I would read Ps.107.... "Oh, that Men would praise God for His goodness, and His wonderful works to the Children of Men"

I would read, and cry, I was thinking, why won't all Mankind just praise God for what He has done for them and jut obey him ,and stop being so rebellious, like the Israelites.

The little Church began to grow, as we went out and made Disciples. for Him. Young married women were born into the Church, and they were all having problems with their husbands. I honestly don't understand why, with my abusive, failed marriage, they would all reach out to me with their problems.

The first was a young Lady named Cora, whose Husband was openly unfaithful to her. When she found out that I was trustworthy, unlike other females she had befriended, we became inseparable. Cora would call me late at night .She would apologize for waking me up, but she had a need and I was there for her.

Other young ladies shared their problems with me. I would lend them a listening ear and offer them comfort, but I never offered any advice when it came to their marriages. That was the Pastor's job. And I told them. So, I would always suggest they go to her. Nevertheless, they would always go to her and say.....I was going through this and that, "and I called Vergie" They had no idea and neither did I, that it appeared that l was trying to take the place of the Pastor. We we all just innocent newborns, happy in Jesus.

Needless to say, God must have used their actions as part of His plan for my life. When His time came for another chapter in my life, I began to feel the Thorns. The Eagle was stirring her nest.

You will read the rest of this episode further on in the book.

My Faith Grows

Sis Banks would give faith building testimonies that would build my faith. It was as if I was watching a movie screen. She had been delivered from breast cancer and once the Lord had spoken to her, telling her to stop taking black draught. She had been taking it for irregularity. He instructed her to drink some olive oil. The next morning, she passed over a hundred gall stones.

That testimony had been before our time. More recently, when she had been instructed of the Lord to build a Church, they had bought and paid for the lumber and the Company, or individual they had purchased it from, failed to deliver. She took him to court. She prayed to God one last time, on the court date. She asked him to send angels before them to prepare the way , *one of my request of the Lord every Day.*

After hearing from both sides the Judge announced to the man, "you must think I'm crazy if you think I'm going to sit here and let you take these poor people's money" The Man was a Caucasian. Back in the nineteen sixties, you would have to agree it was God answering her prayers

I experienced so many favors of God in those early days of my walk with Him. It was so easy to have faith for everything. sis Banks taught " Divine Healing" we trusted God alone for our healing.

By now, I was no longer working at the Sheraton . I was doing domestic work which paid more by the hour. My sister Betty was here now, and we were both riding the bus together. We were coming home one afternoon, and I began having this excruciating pain in my ear and began to moan. My sister looked in my ear and let out a scream and said, "I aint' never seen nothing like that before."

"What comes up with her comes out of her mouth."

"We made it to Sis Banks, she prayed for me and I went home. When I woke up the next morning, I felt nothing, no pain at all. Ok! I expected that, because I knew God would do what He said He would do. But I looked for what it was that was supposed to come out of my ear. The pillow was supposed to be messed up. There was nothing. My faith went up another notch.

I was selected to form a choir. I took piano lessons and played. That little Choir sang under the anointing of the Holy Spirit. I later taught piano lessons in my home, and I formed a group with my boys, we were simply called the ' *Iglus Family.*' We entered a radio singing contest and won the prize, a whole case of peanut butter. We sang at church and a few other places, but my boys grew up and our group broke up. This broke my heart. I grieved over this for a long time.

Oh! How I longed to worship and praise God in this way.

Long after my experience of being born again, and as I grew in the word of God, I learned how God's plan He executed in the Old Testament was being revealed in the New Testament. The types, and the shadows of, God's perfect plan was being fulfilled.

When the animals were brought to the altar of sacrifice to be slain, they struggled, their flesh did not want to die. When the devil spoke to me and told me what would happen if I gave my life to Christ, I was scared. Why would the thought of not being able to enjoy the ugly, nasty, sinful things of the flesh scare you? Because you have one soul, and the devil is gambling for it. Just like he told Eve in the garden, "Don't listen to God, you won't die. God is jealous. Just eat." (paraphrased). I am so glad that I didn't obey him. That I struggled only for a moment, but this flesh had to be placed on the altar and die.

The word of God is undeniably authentic and pure. No one will ever be able to explain it away. It would amaze me when speakers and preachers would come to our church, many years later and testify of when they were drawn to get up from the pew and give their lives to God, and they couldn't move. This would build my faith, and let me know just as Paul told Agrippa, "This thing was not done in a corner."

59

This is a wonderful, life changing, supernatural experience that everyone will have when they submit themselves to God.

Sister and Brother Banks were in the process of having their house foundation raised to build their church beneath. God had instructed her to do this, when she could not find a suitable piece of land to build on. She said God told her, "You already have the land." While the building was in process, they moved out of their house temporarily and moved into Iola's little house next door. It was next to the Church, and they would be able to oversee the work.

Iola moved in with the boys and I temporarily. She and I would stay up practically all night "eating the word." We had found a treasure house in the Word of God. We were feasting on manna from heaven. We both had to get up and go to work at the hotel the next day, and would be worn to a pulp, but it was worth it.

The little church grew, and I grew closer and closer to my Lord. It was still very hard to make ends meet. I was a proud mother. I wouldn't make my needs known to anyone. But there were the times when we didn't have food, Sis Banks and her husband would show up at the gate with a bag of groceries. The Lord was providing, just like he said he would.

Sister Banks found us a little apartment on Galvez street that was for rent with a friend of hers, Mrs. Lawrence. I was very excited to move from midtown to the Ninth Ward now we could walk to church, instead of taking the bus.

I was still desperate, trying to make ends meet. There was no money for food or clothes for myself and the boys. Even though I was living for God, the times were very hard. Even with this being true, it did not matter. I was so on fire for God, just the thought of getting through the day and getting to church on Tuesday night, and to Sunday Service, made it all worthwhile.

The apartment we lived in, was in the back of the main house of my landlady. We were always in the back. She owned some cats. Her back porch was between her house and our apartment. She would leave leftover table food for the cats, and one day I caught my youngest son eating from the cat's dish. This broke my heart.

Our Sunday meals were always "special." as there was a little grocery store right next door. Every Sunday morning , I would walk over and buy a pound of rice, a pound of smoke sausage, and a can of corn. That was our Sunday dinner.

There was this mysterious looking man who owned the grocery store he would always try to rub my hand when I paid for my groceries. Before coming to the Lord, men from all walks of life would admire me. It was all about my body. Before Christ those comments were well received. But in reading my Bible I discovered that if a man lusted after a woman he committed adultery in his heart. Read the account in **Matthew 5:25 (KJV).**

Well! I was not about to cause no man to go to hell lusting after me, I was sold out, I was committed, and determined to obey God's word.

After a hard day's work and waiting on the buses I would come home at night and wash our clothes. I would hang them on the clothesline outside. I was ashamed for people to see them because they were full of holes. But at least they would be clean and white. I would make sure of that.

A washer or dryer did not exist in our home. I had to wash clothes on a washboard, in a washtub in the bathroom. One night I came home worn to a frazzle and I preceded to do my laundry. I was determined that my clothes had to be white. I mixed Clorox and ammonia together. It was a cold night and the heater was on in the bathroom. I was breathing in the fumes from the mixture, but determined to finish, I kept on washing.

All of a sudden I was suffocating and managed to run to a window, open it, and stuck my head out. I had to gasp for breath and made this wheezing noise. The boys were in the other room, and upon hearing the commotion ran into the room.

My boys had learned to have faith in God as well as myself. I heard Lawrence, my oldest boy say, "the devil is trying to kill Mama."

William answered in his deep husky voice, "If he kills her, we'll still have a Mommy, cause Jesus can heal the sick and raise the dead."

One day while living in this apartment showed Walter showed up. I was always a little afraid he would stalk me like all of the other times. But when he realized that my life was truly changed, he never bothered me again. He had long ago moved on with his life with another women, named Jessie Mae, they had two boys together.

The next news I received of him was that he had been killed in a hunting accident. He and a friend had gone hunting, when the friend accidently shot him mistaking him for a deer. I could hardly believe my ears after hearing the news.

How tragic! The service was held at the funeral home. The boys and I attended.

The Letter

As I mentioned earlier, I was a proud individual from very young.

So, after I left Walter, I didn't let my family back home know that he and I were separated, and what a very hard time I was having trying to make it in New Orleans with my boys. Then about a year later, I was inspired to write to my sister Monkey, not a complaint, but as a victorious testimony. This is when I knew that God had anointed me to write.

I began to write and as the pen flew across the pages, the tears flowed. I told her of my struggles, the hardships, the abuse, the separation, but most of all I told her how I had found this brand new life in Christ. I told her that God was taking care of me and my boys and there was no man involved. I told her how God knew when we needed food, and He would miraculously provide for us.

I wrote, and wrote ,and wrote, and the tears kept flowing blotting the paper as I wrote. I could not stop. My hand would not stop moving until the anointing lifted. I have since had many more experiences of that sort.

My sister Betty later told me that Monkey asked her, "Do you believe that Verge is telling the truth about her not having a Man?"

Well, my TESTIMONY was effective on both my sisters, Betty and Earvie. Betty was now married with three children. She and her husband Marvin would join a group of workers who would go to New York each summer to work on the "Muck" this is where they grew vegetables out of season, and recruited workers from different states to harvest them.

While in this process , Betty told me of a dream she had where I was walking through the Morgan quarters with an open Bible in my hand, reading the word. She said she was walking in my footsteps. She vowed right then and there ,"One day, I'm going to New Orleans and get saved." And she did.

Physically Blind

I don't remember what lead up to what took place in my life next. But one day just as suddenly as it had happened with my ear, my eyes became irritated and infected. I became blind in both eyes. But never stopped going to church. My friend Cora would come to the back apartment and escort me to her car and bring me to Church.

I had to wear a blindfold over my eyes. I would go to church, stand up in that choir and I would sing my heart out. I was so in love with Jesus, nothing could stop me from serving him. Even in the house I had to be blind folded.. And even a little stream of light coming through the window would cause excruciating pain. We had to keep the windows covered with dark curtains at all times.

Sister Banks would pray for me constantly. The pain was unbearable but I was determined to wait on God. Sis Banks decided I needed more help since I had the kids to take care of. My sister Betty was in New York working on the muck. Sis Banks secured an address somehow, and reached out to her to come to New, Orleans to help me.

Betty being one always willing to drop everything to help, made plans to leave that next Saturday but her husband Marvin, fell off of a truck that Friday. He had   a concussion and was unconscious for eighteen days. So, she could not come at that time. God had another plan. Every single night I would proclaim "Tomorrow, I will see her."

But the next morning, it was the same I could not see. But I never stopped believing. In fact, it seemed to get. worse. One day, I felt something under my eyelids as if it was some kind of growth. It felt rough, and scratchy. I sensed the devil was telling me , "So, you're waiting on God to heal your eyes, when you're really going blind for good"

But that did not scare me like he intended. I believed God was going to do what he said he would do, and give me my sight back. God saw my faith, and he honored it. For the bible says in **James 2: 14-26 (KJV)**... What does it profit, my brethren, if someone says he has faith but does not have works.

He spoke explaining to me to mix a solution of warm water and a little Epsom salt, and use it as drops to put in my eyes. I had never heard of this before. But I obeyed. I pulled my eyelids open and put in the drops I told myself as I did every other night "Tomorrow I will see!"

The next morning, when I moved my eyelid over my eyeballs it felt smooth, not rough and scratchy like before, but smooth, like glass. I knew! I just knew I had passed this test. God had found me faithful.

I quickly went to the mirror. Pried my eye open, and I could see. There was a glossy raised surface on my eyeball, as if someone had smoothed off the roughness. I was overcome with joy. I ran to the phone and called Sis Banks. I couldn't talk for crying tears of joy, and praising God. Yes! He had done it once more. My children heard the commotion and came peeping to see what was going on. I heard them whispering one to another, Mama can see. No more getting away with mischief. God had done what he said he would do. He had healed me. Everywhere I went, I had this awesome testimony that God had given me back my sight. So many were blessed, and some gave their lives to Christ because of it.

The Visit From God

I was doing domestic work at this time, standing in the hot sun waiting for the bus and changing buses. I would be dog tired but nothing kept me away from church. That was my sanctuary, it was a small church and congregation, but we were family. The Power of God would fall in that place like Heaven on Earth.

One Sunday after service, I was taking a nap as always, since we were not going home with the Milsaps. I had an open vision, whatever it was it was not a dream, I am sure of that.

All of a sudden I heard this strong voice saying, "Be not afraid. I am the Lord your God. I will hold you in my right hand, I will not leave thee nor will I forsake thee.

The voice was as it was extended right above my head. In midair. I jerked myself to turn over to see who it was. When I did, a light brighter than any light I had ever seen, stabbed me in my eyes. I was afraid, but the anointing fell upon me and I began to speak in that heavenly language. I called Sis Banks and told her of my experience, and then I wrote it down.

I had many encounters similar to that one. There would be times when I would be praying in a dark room and it seemed that God Himself would come into the room and it caused me to be fearful. But I know he had sent His angels to minister to me in those very hard times. I often had dreams of being caught up in midair with Him, and this would bring me such joy. God would speak to me so plainly he brought His word , and I took him at His word.

The Word of God Speaks

I remember the time I had decided to get help from the Welfare Department. I always took my bible wherever I went. As I was on my way, riding the bus, I was reading **Heb. 13:5** , and the part of the verse that says," be content with what you have for God for I will never leave you, never will I forsake you."

I knew without a doubt, God was speaking to me. I thought, "I can get off his bus, and take another one back home. I said to the Lord in my mind, "but Lord, I don't have anything to be content with." But I had placed my life in his hands, and he knew what was best for me. I knew women who were on welfare and had a man living in the house. The welfare representative would come to do inspection, and they would hide the man's clothes under the bed until the Rep left. I was living for God and that was not his plan for me.

An Open Vision

One Sunday afternoon I was asleep and had an open vision. It was as if I was wide awake. The man from the Grocery store was coming through the back window. He made it to my room, I was frightened to death. I struggled to move, to get out of his way, if he touches me, Even if I go to the Altar and repent, I will never be clean again, and the Holy Ghost won't dwell in me "no! no! stop!.

He made it to my bed. With all the strength I could muscle up I jerked myself away from him, and I woke up. Thank God! it was only a dream!

Hurricane Betsy

That same year, 1965, a major hurricane named Betsy hit New Orleans. My boys and I went to Sister Wilson's, a church members, home for safety. After we were there for a little while, Sis Banks called and told us to get out in a hurry. It was alleged that the city had broken the levy to allow the water to come to the Ninth ward.

Thank God for one of Sister Wilson's in- laws who owned a dump truck and took us to a shelter. The water was rising rapidly, and I had

Kendrick , my youngest in my arms ,and the others by the hands, and we were running for our lives.

The water quickly rising to my waist. Sister Wilson's daughter and son- in- law lived just a block away which was a blessing. We made it to Holy Cross School in the dump truck which was one of the shelters.

Sis Banks, Iola and Brother Banks ended up across the river at the naval base. We were separated, and I hated it. But I put on a brave face and testified to everyone in that shelter, how God had healed my eyes.

The campus at Holy Cross looked like a river for days. The water was almost to the second floor window. When the waters receded they finally started allowing people to come back to the Ninth Ward.

Sister Banks sent Brother Banks to see about us, when it was safe to do so, they transferred us all to the base. I was so happy to be reunited with my spiritual family as there were many lost lives. We lost everything, including my big upright piano with the rich beautiful sound.

After the Storm

After Hurricane Betsy, the boys and I settled in and we lived in several different houses. It seemed like everywhere we went, trouble followed. One house that was half of a duplex had a family with three boys. They were like Satan himself. Once, when I had shopped for my boys school supplies and uniforms ,and put them away until time for school the boys next door broke our door and destroyed everything I bought. They spread the school supplies and clothes all over the floor, and poured the black shoe polish that I had bought for their shoes, all over them. I was devastated. The parents had no control over them, and made no effort to discipline them.

This was another storm we had to face. Sis Banks prayed with me for Gods' guidance, and protection, that He would lead us to a safe place to live. A duplex right across the street, in front of the Church became available. The family in the other half consisted of a husband, his wife, and one half grown son.

The son was an unholy terror. He harassed my boys while I was at work. When I washed my clothes, I hung them on the clothesline in the backyard to dry. Every time, he would pull them off and throw them all over the ground.

One day I came home from my domestic work to find my baby boy, Kendrick with a double nose. His eyes were bruised and swollen shut. The boy next door had hit him across the face with a broomstick. I was devastated my heart was broken to see my baby this way.

It left a wound in my heart for a long time. I felt so helpless, and so hopeless. I had to work to take care of my boys, but I needed to be home to protect them.

It was not long after that incident my neighbors son joined the military and died. I don't believe it was in action, but from some other

Oh! How I needed God's help. Every time I thought about it, I cried. It was a mini version of the grief I felt after William's death. This was it. I could not leave my boys alone anymore. I had to protect them. Because, I heard it was a possible overdose. My heart grieved for his parents, that was their only child.

Shortly afterwards Betty's dream was fulfilled. After the 'Muck' season was over in New York Marvin dropped my sister Betty off in New Orleans and went on to Georgia to take care of some business. He later joined she and the children in New Orleans.

They lived with us until they found a place of their own. I was ecstatic to have my family with me. Marvin lived diligently for God until he passed away in 2013.

My sister Betty, and most of her family is still living for in God in Holiness. And before my sister Monkey passed away in 1986, she acknowledged that what I shared with her in the letter was real.

The Warts

Another thing that happened that sent my faith rocketing . Before I gave my life to Christ, my right hand was covered with black warts that were formed like birds nest. I mean covered. There was no clear place on my hand to be found. The warts were round with little edges that looked like a bird nest would look.   And they had little round molds inside of them that looked like little eggs.

Once when I was at an appointment at Charity Hospital I showed them to the doctor and asked how could I get rid of them. He snapped at me without looking at them and said, " I don't know, I don't have em."

What could I say back in those days I just kept doing what I had been doing? When I went to the store or whenever I had to reach for something, I would extend my left hand when I reached for change as I was ashamed of my right one.

After I was baptized and filled with the Holy Ghost, I don't know when or where but one day I looked at my right hand, and it was made clean, just like when Jesus cleansed the lepers. He had cleansed my hand. I remember what I said when I saw it, " Now I have holy hands." God was getting the glory out of my life.

Reflection

Iola and I would do special little things for Sister Banks, like cooking meals. One Christmas we were having she and Brother Banks over to the house for dinner and Iola was doing the turkey. Well when everything was done and ready to serve, Iola preceded to carve the turkey. When she took it out of the pan the giblets were still packed in their wrapping stuck in the neck opening . She had made a mixture of cornmeal and water and poured it inside the turkey. We laugh about it whenever we get the chance to talk. We had some really good times together.

Mary Castille

I worked in a private residence in Chalmette, Louisiana which is in St. Bernard Parish, cleaning house for a white woman named   Mary Castille. Apparently she had never heard that slavery had ended. She instructed me to use the garage to change out of my street clothes into my uniform. "Make sure to use the toilet in the garage, "she instructed me. Also, she gave me a special glass to drink out of, and one particular dish to eat lunch from. She would give me leftover food to bring home for the kids, but, it was always put into an empty can. Yes! A vegetable can.

I despised what she was doing, but for now, I had to hold my peace, and bite my tongue. This was the only means I had to take care of my boys, so I did whatever was asked of me.

However, I witnessed to her, as I did to everyone else I met. I told her of the healing power of God. And how he had healed my eyes and many other miracles he had performed through the prayers of Sister Banks.

Every single time I had to take the bus to her house, I would stand at the bus stop and boohoo . This was so unfair.

My oldest son, Walter was old enough to do yard work, so she asked me to bring him with me on occasions to help out. When he would get thirsty, and asked for water, I informed her that he wanted water, and her response was that he drink from the water hose.

Again, I felt trapped. Why did I have to subject my children to this type of treatment. I was hurt and felt helpless and hopeless for a moment. Then I remembered the promises of God, and I knew one day he would deliver us just as he had delivered the children of Israel from there bondage. Mary owned a beauty shop uptown and also some rental properties. There were rooms that she rented out

to single men. Mary needed hired help to clean the rooms, so she asked me to help.

One day while I was cleaning one of the rooms the tenant came in. I don't know what he was on, but that monster cornered me. He held me against the bed and the wall, and with all the strength I could muster up I used it to get away from him.

Well, you guessed it. I reported it to both Mary and her Mom and that was the last time I showed my face at that place. While I was still working for Mrs. Mary she developed a terrible rash on her lower body. Nothing she did, nor what the doctor's recommended would get rid of that rash

Well, like Naaman, in the Bible she remembered my testimony about God's power, and had me make an appointment for her with

Sister Banks for prayer. She went to the Church and met with Sister Banks and was healed of that awful rash. Won't God do it.? What a God, what a God!! You know he had a plan, a perfect plan. Soon after this episode, I was recommended for a job in a private home as a cook. I was elated. I was overcome with joy. God had heard, and answered my prayer. I was leaving the slave house.

But there was the time when she went in her bathroom and found her toilet seat up and asked me if I had used her toilet.

I humbly answered her "yes, but I let the seat up. I don't want to catch what you have either."

I reminded her of how God had favored her, and healed her of that awful rash. I honestly didn't know if I was in the Spirit, or if it was my flesh, but I know I had a lot of hurt, built up that I had to get out.

I expressed my feelings about, every single thing that I was displeased with, the special glass, the special dish, changing my clothing in the garage, the food in the vegetable cans, drinking water from the water hose.

She told me that she didn't know any better. She thought that this was the way it was done, because this was what her mother taught her.

She explained the water situation as following. "Everybody knows that you don't drink cold water when you're hot." Maybe she was right about that. I never did question it. I did not resent her as a person. But the treatment was unacceptable . Maybe if I had spoken up earlier, things would have turned out differently, or maybe it was just that God had another plan.

She sincerely regretted my leaving her, but it was too late. My sister Betty took my place for a while before she got a job at the sewing factory.

The last job I had was in a private home as a cook for a wealthy family who lived in Metairie, Louisiana. They had a lady who was the Nanny, and the Housekeeper. I didn't choose any particular one to witness to or give my testimony to anyone who crossed my path got an ear full.

When I testified to the housekeeper and told her God had delivered me from adultery she quickly responded, "Yeah right! You've turned to women." Like the babe I was in Christ, again, I ran to Sister Banks heartbroken to be accused of such a thing.

As always, she would get out the bible and comfort me, and reassure me with the word of God.

Others would tell me, "Yeah, right! You know you got your midnight riders!!" To get to the different jobs, I had to take the bus. Sometimes it was in the broiling hot sun, and other times in the freezing cold. I was having back problems . I would reach for the next hedge growing along the street to help me walk. I never complained, I just did what I had to do to take care of my boys.

PART THREE

My Career with Stanley

I had been seeking employment that would allow me to be available to my children and still make a living for them. One day when I was searching the newspaper ads I found one where you could work from home.

I came across an advertisement by Stanley Home Products seeking people for jobs as direct sales representatives. I had never done anything like this before. But I was willing to try anything to protect my boys.

I asked my Pastor what she thought about it and she said it would not hurt for me to try. I called the number and Virginia Thomas, a Stanley sales manager, came right over with my sales kit. She was supposed to 'issue' it. That is when you deliver the starter kit to a potential dealer, sit and unpack it. Go over all of the material, explaining everything to them. But Virginia sat the kit down on the floor, collected her three dollars, and left.

Yes ! three dollars, which I had borrow from my neighbor.

Virginia was my leader since I answered her ad , but the Branch Manager, was Bonnie Deason. There were two branches in New Orleans, both in the same office building on Jefferson Highway.

So, began my Stanley career. I had no experience, whatsoever. Well, there I was, green as grass, as ignorant to this as all outdoors, getting ready to begin my new career. It was suppose, to be Virginia's job to train me, but I began on this adventure, relying on the information I gathered from the manual included in the kit.

The concept was to convince a lady of a household to invite at least three other ladies into her home to allow you, the Stanley dealer, to come in and demonstrate your premiums and products, with the primary purpose to sell your product. In the business world you became a leader because you had the ability to train and build up people to promote and sell products.

I didn't know a soul. Iola, my friend, whom I had followed to the little prayer room where I got saved. Iola had a cousin who had a grocery store and we asked her if she would host a party. She said yes!

The guests were all gathered ,and it was time for me to begin. They were all there, staring me right in the face. I could hear my knees knocking . After every word I said I had to clear my throat and wipe my hands down my face. First, I had to thank the Hostess for inviting me and her friends into her home.

Next I had to tell the Stanley Story. When I had learned the story I was overwhelmed with joy. Stanley was founded upon religious principles. Mr. Frank Stanley Beverage was a religious man who cared about people.

The years from 1929, through 1939, were known as the Years of the Great Depression. In 1935, (the year I was born) he took his life savings and invested in a company so men could have jobs, since they were all out of work.

Now, I knew it was God's will for me to be a part of this company. It did not start out as a party plan, but with men that went from door to door selling the product.

The party plan was adopted in 1937. One day a salesman went to a home and found several ladies in that one home. He discovered he could sell more to a group that one person and that began the party plan.

I booked three parties from Pam's, my hostess. She had a great crowd and I was on my way. One of the ladies was Sister Viola Watson, the Mother of Pastor Raymond Watson of the Apostolic Outreach Center. She was a schoolteacher and not yet saved

It was not long before I became comfortable with making a presentation before the hostesses and their guests. I would play a game or two that would have them laughing so hard they would be falling on the floor. I had always believed in being the very best at what task I took on."

The bible says in **Ecclesiastes 9:10**… Whatever your hands find to do, do it with all you might.

Everything I did was guided by His hand. My prayer was always. that He would order my steps in His word, that he would lead me in a right path whatever I attempted to do.

There was another method we used to book parties. We went from door to door with a premium in our hands and knocked on the door and hoped to get invited in to demonstrate it to gain a party.

Many successful businesses are built on the biblical principle. I applied the following principle to my business.

"Do unto others as you would have them do unto you. "**Luke 6:30 (NIV)**

I learned how to hold the guest interest with the premiums. When I finished demonstrating an item, they felt like they just have to have it, so they couldn't wait to book their party, get started on their outside sales so they would qualify for their prize.

I would do the same with the products. I used sales pitches that would be funny, and get them laughing, relaxed. But I never used a sales pitch that was a lie, as so many do today in order to gain a profit. For the Bible says (the love of money is the root of all evil). I upheld my integrity. I remained honest in all of my dealings with people. I quickly moved up the the Stanley ladder to the next level..

God caused me to prosper like I never had before. There were times I would arrive at a party, and had to spend thirty to forty-five minutes preparing outside orders that the hostess had collected. This all meant a larger profit for me . I had so many sales, I couldn't handle them. When the truck delivered my shipment, there was no space in the living room floor to place them.

I remember the time I was so overwhelmed with boxes that I just broke down and cried. We had to unbox and separate each hostesses order, and bag every customers order. And in addition to verbally witnessing everywhere I went, I placed a gospel tract in every single bag that went out, and God prospered me financially in a way that was unbelievable to the unbeliever.

My boys would help me, and at the age of fifteen, my oldest Lawrence began making deliveries and collections for me all over the city .

I won't dare attempt to write about my forty-five plus years of my Stanley career, but I absolutely loved it. So, I will just hit on the highlights. I just loved meeting new people, I enjoyed witnessing to everyone who would listen

I had heard that once you became a Stanley Dealer you dreamed "degreaser," Stanley's # one product. Yes, I loved, loved , loved it, but still loved God more.

There were certain areas in New Orleans that were credited for being more prejudice than others. There was St Bernard Parish, Chalmette, Metairie, and the Kenner area.

Well, I went into homes from one end of New Orleans to the other going from the projects to the riches homes. Everyone treated me the same. When I went to a home where the husband was at home, he would run out to the car ,instead of the hostess, to help me bring my display of premiums, and products' inside. He treated me as if it was a blessing to have me there.

After the party was over, I would be the first one the hostesses served refreshments.

It has been said that "One bad apple can spoil a whole barrel," meaning that one person, element, thing, etc. can ruin the entire group, situation or project.

That may be true of apples, but I disagree when it comes to people. Many folk will judge a church or a group by their experience with one person. Some will even go by the opinions of others, not encountering an experience for themselves.

When I fell in love with Jesus, I fell in love with people. God is love and He loves all mankind. He is no respecter of people. In the world that we live in, everyone is different, every situation is different. I refuse to allow anyone to come to me and start a conversation referring to a particular church, or a group, and brand them as "They."

Our former Pastor Danny Brown would always say, "People are People everywhere you go. There is no perfect Church, there is no perfect Person, only a perfect God." I have been treated like a rattlesnake by some of my own race, but treated like royalty by another race. God is love

Church Hurt

The Church grew and I grew with it. Our children grew up finished school, and started moving on. What I'm about to write is just to reveal how the devil will present himself in the midst of God's work. God was using me, and Satan began to sow the seed of discord, a spirit of jealousy rose up its ugly head in the church. But as we know, Satan is an accuser of the Brethren.

This was the first time I experienced "Church hurt." I would go around testifying to everyone that I met that our little church was perfect, and everyone in it, and dared them to claim any different. I was young in the Lord back then. I would not have done anything contrary to the word of God, I loved Him too much, and I loved my pastor, my sisters and brothers.

Cora, and her two sisters were very close to me, even though we were all family. Eventually Satan convinced them to shun me by telling them not to talk to me because all I wanted was their business.

They all did just that. I didn't know what had taken place, but I was crushed, my heart was so broken.it was devastating.

There was another sister that also confided in me and clung to me, she would come to my house and her little girl would jump up and down on my bed. She wouldn't say a word, and neither would I. I never wanted to hurt people's feeling.   If I had cooked when she came over and I had cooked beans, she would tell me, "I'm tired of beans, I want okra" I would run and grab okra and cook it for her. We were family, that was what I was supposed to do. We were all young in the Lord.

Well, she stood out and told me what had been suggested to all of them by a responsible source. But she was not going along with it, because that is what the people in the world do.

Some people will say "I don't need to know." Well, I'm the opposite, I need to know. It helps me to make some kind of sense out of why a thing is done, and maybe bring some kind of closure. Don't just leave me hanging.

Time went on, and things got worse. I was accused of taking over the church. It got to the place where I dreaded going to church. I was hurt, I was depressed. I was lonely. I would cry every time. I would ask God, why, I told Him " God you know my heart, you would let me know if I was doing these things, wouldn't you? Why God, why? Like Hezekiah, I would turn my face to the wall and cry.

One time when this was going on, I cried out" Why God, why." God said to me clearly, not verbally but clearly, "It's a Saul spirit" I knew what he was referring to, the time Saul sought to take David's life because of God's anointing upon him.

One of the sisters that was shunning me was going to have a baby. Out of the clear blue, she called me and said," Vergie, you're my sister, and I am not going to shun you. I tell you the word of God spoke to my precious sister that day. The word of God takes precedence over the advice or instruction of any leader or authority. There is no such thing as any true man or woman of God giving advice that is contrary to his word.

My sister obeyed the voice of God, as the Apostles did in their ministry. She went on to tell me that she was going to the hospital. They were going to induce labor. They delivered the baby, but something went wrong. The water entered her lungs and she lingered for a few days but didn't make it.

Pastor Banks and I went together to visit her. Within a day or two, she went on to receive her heavenly reward.

My Branch

Stella was my second Stanley Home Products manager; she was from the deep South of Alabama and a Caucasian.

I became a " pro" I booked parties from parties, from door to door, made the free gifts so desirable, that people were asking me for parties. I became so good at it, Customers we're saying "Vergie, you could sell ice to an Eskimo." I made more money than I had ever seen. I quickly moved up from dealer to Group leader with Dealers under me. Then I climbed to the next level, Unit Sales Leader, with Groups and Dealers.

I held sales meetings in my home and trained them to sell Stanley products and recruit Dealers. They also learned how to book parties.

We had so much fun. we would meet up and split up in groups of twos and go knocking on doors. Just like I would go out with my Church to pass out gospel tracts.

We offered them a gift just for inviting at least three friends or neighbors over to see a demonstration of premiums and products. If they said yes, we would build on that, and offer a second gift if they could get ten people to attend.

Many accepted but we were turned down by some. We had a set time to meet back up for lunch and to report our progress. Some of the Dealers were scared to death to knock on doors. When we met we would fall on the ground laughing about some of the responses we received from the people who had refused.

Once my partner and I knocked on a door and a big, burly man came to the door. I asked, "May I speak to your wife"? He growled back, I'm the Wife" We laughed about that for years to come.

With Stella, it was not just about production. She was, and still to this day, is a real true friend. I was like family. Stella has three daughters, Cheryl, Jennifer, and Daphne that all just grafted me in as family.

Then there was Connie, a Stanley dealer from England and her husband, Mike along with their son Mike Jr., who was engaged to Cheryl all of them becoming like my family.

Ecclesiastes: 9- 10 says, Whatsoever thy hand findth to do, do it with all thy might: for there is no work, nor device, nor knowledge, nor wisdom, in the grave wither thou goeth. And that is how I have lived my life.

Recognition, prizes and a lot of hoop-la were given for a job well done. Being the Branch Manager, Stella was the one to hand out all these at the Monday morning sales meetings, and I was always the one receiving them. I was the top producer.

There was jealousy among the other dealers, not only because Stella took a stand as a Branch Manager, but because she treated me as an equal. One Monday morning, one of the dealers became so angry, all because I was black, and good at what I was doing. She went after Stella, and the others had to hold her back literally. Jealousy is as cruel as the grave.

After a while, Stella got appointed to another branch in Pensacola, Florida. Because of my record, I was next in line to take over the New Orleans Branch.

My superiors thought this was a bad idea. The area manager, Mr. Herb Lanier called a meeting with me. He explained that if I became the Manager of the existing Branch, I would be "crucified." Instead the officials decided that they would take my Group and create a new branch Thus, we became the Crescent City Branch.

They appointed another dealer who was a good recruiter, but was also resentful of me, because I did a better job than she. My Branch set up an office in the same office building as the other two. Soon afterward,

Stanley Home products adapted the plan to move all offices into the homes of the managers. As a branch manager you had to maintain an office, and a secretary. When Stella moved to Pensacola, her daughter Cheryl became my secretary.

When Cheryl had to give up her position I appointed Connie, her mother-in-law, who had also joined my branch when Stella left to become my secretary.

In addition to being co-workers Stella and I became best friends. When she moved to Pensacola we held branch meeting there. I would drive over and she would invite me to spend the night, her daughter Daphne would give up her bed for me. In the morning she would fix breakfast for me as if I was a special guest.

Read James 2:1-26 :

My brethren have not the faith of our Lord Jesus Christ, the Lord of glory, with respect of persons. Show no partiality as you hold the faith in our Lord Jesus Christ, the Lord of glory. For if a man wearing a gold ring and fine clothing comes into your assembly, and a poor man in shabby clothing also comes in, and if you pay attention to the one who wears the fine clothing and say, "You sit here in a good place," while you say to the poor man, "You stand over there," or, "Sit down at my feet," have you not then made distinctions among yourselves and become judges with evil thoughts? Listen, my beloved brothers, has not

God chosen those who are poor in the world to be rich in faith and heirs of the kingdom, which he has promised to those who love him.

After managing the Pensacola Branch for a while, Stella left Stanley for a season. After six years, she moved back to New Orleans and back to Stanley. She did all kinds of promotions, bringing me right along with her. I always found myself doing some new thing with Stella, and it was fun.

We fried fish and shrimp in Dillard's Department Stores, passing out samples with the primary purpose of selling the product. The company would give you the pot and I still have mine to this day. It's still the best one I have, this was around 1975.

Stella had all kinds of connections. If she would have had the knowledge and the know-how, I would have been a BIG time gospel singer way back then.

But "God had another plan."

She would "book "me to perform on stages that were set up in the surrounding malls . I would get requests from the songs of Mahalia Jackson to songs like, "Old Man Rivers."

Another thing she got us into was promoting Kayak Swimming pools. We would go from one mall to another signing up people to purchase swimming pools.

By now, I had no problem convincing people to buy anything I had to sell, and I just loved meeting and talking, and witnessing to people.

But there was one stipulation, I had to believe in the product I was selling.

No gimmicks, no false advertisement. If I didn't believe it would do what it was designed to do, it was not going to come out of my mouth. Stella even got us a job changing out greeting cards in drug stores.

The boys had grown up to be young men. Until they became teenagers, I had never even allowed them to spend the night with anyone. I was so attached to them. I was known as " the Lady with the three little Boys" by those who didn't know me personally.

I would win many of the prizes Stanley offered. When there were trips to be won, I would win two or three. That meant I could invite two or more guest to come. Once I won three trips to Panama City, Florida, and took my son Kendrick, and my niece, Gwen along. Not only had I declared that I would not ever fly, but that I'd never go out in deep water. The deepest I had been was at the edge of the beach on an inner tube in Apalachicola ,while working for the Morgan family on the farm.

On one of the side trips to Panama City we went on a fishing trip. I was afraid to go on the boat, but Kendrick and Gwen wanted to go, and I wasn't about to let them go alone. Remember, I am the person who puts everyone else before myself.

So, on the boat we went. It was a houseboat, that made it a little better. There was a contest, and guess who won? I caught the biggest fish on the boat. I loved the competition. I just knew with the help of God, I could accomplish anything I set my heart to do and I was spreading His word as I went, witnessing, testifying, and placing tracts in every bag.

I began my traveling adventure. There were two things I was apprehensive about. First of all, I was not at all excited about leaving my boys alone.

Lawrence was the quiet one not as outgoing like William, and not as popular. I noticed his shyness, and lack of confidence. I wanted him to feel loved, and excepted as well as the other two boys, and not feel left out.

William was a member of the School Choir. At the end of his senior year, they planned a senior trip to Texas. Their music teacher gave the parents the option of making their suits, or hiring a seamstress to make them. I opted to make Williams. The suits were of a royal blue textured material, I made an identical one for Lawrence, but in a rust color. I paid the fee and sent him on the senior trip with William's school choir.

Lawrence had graduated from Carver High and had started attending Delgado Community College taking up Auto Mechanic's. I remember asking him why he had chosen that particular "greasy" field. He kindly answered, "that money ain't greasy" Later, because of some technicality with my social security, he dropped out, and got a job at LSU Dental School where he became a manager in the maintenance depart

The next year, William graduated from Nicholas High School. He was very popular in school. He had a dark complexion and my features.

He could have dated any girl he wanted. He was smart, and comical in a serious kind of way. He had this way of saying something funny and never cracking a smile.

One time there seemed to be an epidemic of mosquitos. they were all on the screens. William made the statement, "They got enough mosquitos to make mosquito soup." He knew how to rebuke the devil. One day I had cooked a pot of something, maybe beans with pickle meat, or maybe ham hocks. I was lying down resting in my room. I heard William saying, "no devil! no devil!" I asked who was he talking to , he said " The devil is trying to make me go in that pot and eat the meat out of it, and I'm telling him no" .

William was also hotheaded and daring. He was not afraid of anything. After he graduated from high school, he just could not seem to find his place in life. He had big dreams and wanted to become a music artist. He was self-taught musician and learned to play several musical instruments, and when he had written a few songs he was ready to pursue his career. But he needed money.

I don't know if any mother could have been more protective of her children. As Jesus said ,"O Jerusalem, Jerusalem, the city that kills the prophets and stones those who are sent to it! How often would I have gathered your children together as a hen gathers her brood under her wings, and you were not willing! **"Matt:23:37 (KJV).** So, this is what I did for my boys. " There were times when I would try to imagine if I would be able to survive if anything would happen to either one of my boys. some evenings I would be dog tired after work, and the children would be playing outside. I couldn't hardly keep my eyes open, but I would force myself to stay awake, because I would not go to sleep with my boys outside, and I was not going to deprive them of their playtime.

I use to listen to Evangelist Lester Roloff who had a a radio program "Family Altar" that aired on many stations from 1944 to the '80s. I heard this anonymous poem one day and it reminded me of my boys.

"Are all the children in?"

I think oft times as night draws nigh
Of the old farmhouse on the hill,
Of a yard all wide and blossom-starred
Where the children played at will.
And when the night at last came down
Hushing the merry din,
Mother would look around and ask,

"Are all the children in?"
Tis many and many a year since then,
And the house on the hill
No longer echoes to children's feet
And the yard is still, so still.

But I see it all, the shadows creep,
And though many years have been
Since then, I can hear mother ask,
"Are all the children in?"

I wonder if when the shadows fall
On the last short, earthly day,
When we say good-by to the world outside
All tired with our childish play,
When we step out into that other land
Where mother so long has been,
Will we hear her ask, just as of old,
"Are all the children in?

My Stanley Journey Continues

I had gone on many local trips to surrounding cities, like Biloxi, Mississippi, Gulf Port, Mobile, Ala, and Pensacola, Florida. Those places were where our Board meetings for the Branch Managers were held. We would call them " bored " meetings ,because they were so boring. We would sit for hours listening to the same thing that we had heard a hundred times, which were statistics. We always carried plenty of no dose to keep us awake, when the coffee had worn off.

The first time I flew was when I went on our yearly convention to the Home office in Westfield, Massachusetts. We were going to take a flight to Springfield, Massachusetts, where we would be bussed to Westfield. It was just after a plane had crashed .

I had been expressing my fears of flying. Stella used this to point out to me that this was the safest time to fly, right after a plane crashes. She said that all of the airlines would be taking extra precautions . She also pointed out that the news never made a point to report the number of planes that landed safely. This is the first time I had left my boys home alone for a long period of time. The Home offices had given us phone numbers where our families could reach us in case of an emergency.

My Sister Betty drove me to the airport along with her children and my boys. While I was in line waiting to board the plane, my sister had a habit of saying whatever came up out of her mouth ,told my son Lawrence," You better say goodbye to your Momma, this might be the last time you see her"

You would have to know just how concerned and devoted and protective Lawrence was of his mother. My sister did not intend for that to be a negative statement ,but was just being comical. I will say more about this subject later in the book when I talk about, "The Power of the Tongue "

The first plane we boarded was a 747 jet. We took off and it was as if I was sitting in my living room. "Awwww! ,this is not bad at all.

We changed planes in Atlanta, Georgia and boarded what we called a "tub". We started bouncing around, and rocking, and God forgave me, but I promised Him that if He brought me safely back Home, I would never fly again. on the way back we had to circle the Atlanta airport for one hour waiting for a spot to land.

Well. I did not keep my promise. I flew several times after that, and would have a lots of fun with my friend Kathy, while praying.

Well, while I gathered together with thousands of Stanley folk, I get a phone call. I was summoned to the office not knowing what to expect. Lawrence had utilized the phone number left for him to tell me that Kendrick was being disobedient. He really called to make sure I was safe.

Really Good Times With Stanley

My first visit to the Home office was so exciting for me. We were given a tour of the company and the history ,and an explanation of how the products were made.

But the thing that impressed me most was when we got to Mr. Beverages office, there was his huge glass covered desk Underneath the glass were faded scriptures ,in his own handwriting, and old newspaper clippings about his life.

I was just overcome with joy that I had chosen to join this Christian based company.

From the time I joined Stanley, I was asked to lead the singing. Each Branch held weekly sales meeting every Monday Morning. We sang motivational songs that represented Stanley Home Products.

In Westfield, there was a park known as Stanley Park. In the park, was a beautiful garden where flowers grew all year round and in one corner was a rose garden. Mr. Beverage would get up early in the morning and walk among the flowers and pray for his business, and God blessed it abundantly.

His favorite song was *"In The Garden,"* sometimes referred as titled by its first line, " I COME TO THE GARDEN ALONE".

I come to the garden alone

While the dew is still on the roses

And the voice I hear, falling on my ear

The Son of God discloses

And He walks with me

And He talks with me

And He tells me I am His own

And the joy we share as we tarry there

None other has ever known.

He speaks and the sound of His voice

Is so sweet the birds hush their singing

And the melody that He gave to me

Within my heart is ringing

And He walks with me

And He talks with me

And He tells me I am His own

And the joy we share as we tarry there

None other has ever known

I'd stay in the garden with Him

'Though the night around me be falling

But He bids me go, through the voice of woe

His voice to me is calling

And He walks with me

And He talks with me

And He tells me I am His own

And the joy we share as we tarry there

None other has ever known

Charles Austin Miles the composer of this song was a prolific American writer of gospel songs. He is best known for this hymn written in 1912 as he was walking in his garden doing his morning devotions.

On Thursday mornings we would gather around the big oaks in the park and sing . I was always the one to lead the team in song. I never felt special because of this, I felt like I was just doing my duty as a part of the Stanley group.

I won many of my Stanley dealers and hostesses to the Lord, and recruited them as dealers. Up until then, I was the only one in my Zone who was Pentecostal. Stella was a devout Baptist, and believed in the Word of God.

I was now a Branch Manager, bringing some of my groups on trips along with me. Once my District Manager approached me and said to me" Vergie, I've been watching you. In spite of your position, you have never changed". He was speaking of the facts that I hung with my Dealers, instead of hanging with the Branch Managers. To me it all means the same. Whosoever God entrusted to my care, I was to care for and watch over. I did it as a mother, a Grandmother, in some instances, as a Foster Mom, and as a Spiritual Mother.

One year, I went to Westfield as the "First Princess " This meant that I was the second highest in sales, in the entire zone. They would always hold a Gold Cup Banquet for the top salespeople, and we didn't find out who had won until we arrived.

I was pleasantly surprised to discover that I was in the top sales. There was only one person above me, a guy.   As was the custom the three at the top rank each had one of the Home office officials crown them.

Page was crowned as King, then it was my turn to be crowned. We we seated at the head VIP's table which was placed on the stage. My official was Dwight Manners he placed my crown upon my head and kissed me on each cheek.   Can you imagine how weird I felt? But deep down inside I felt a sense of pride at where God had brought me from. Surely this was part of his plan for me!

He had brought me from the Tobacco Fields of Georgia having been beaten and battered by a cruel and abusive husband, and almost being kicked by a white man, to being kissed on the cheek by a white man. After all it was still in the seventies. My friend Martha Book, from Alexandria, was crowned second Princess.

At the Banquet, the custom was that after the meal was finished, and the gold cup had been presented, they brought in dancers to serenade the winners to the tune of soft music.

Well, I knew where to draw the line. Can you believe I refused to dance. I'm sure at this point, they were certain I was weird. There was not a soul there from my church , but I believed it was not the thing for me to participate in, so I refused.   I wanted to make sure I was representing Christ wherever I went and in everything I did. I would rather overdo than to come short. Otherwise those were some really good times.

Cruises

On one of our side trips we went to Washington DC, and got to sit in on the Senate and visited the Statue of Liberty. It was one of the most surreal events seeing the bloodstained pillow where Abraham Lincoln.

There were cruises to be won and again I broke my promise of ever going out in deep water .We went to the Bahama Islands on two occasions. I had good times on every trip. On the first trip we visited Paradise Island, and the home where Sidney Pottier was born and raised. I rode on a glass bottom boat and had fun shopping at the straw market. In 2001, the straw markets burned down.

Another year our side trip was to Boston, Massachusetts. We travelled from Westfield to Boston by bus and spent the night . We ate dinner that night in a cafe facing the ocean. One of my dealers and I ordered none other than blueberry pancakes. Those were the biggest pancakes we had ever seen. They covered a big dinner plate. We couldn't finish eating them.

The next day we toured the city of Boston. I was so impressed with all of that history. We toured places where the Boston Tea Party took place on the "Old Ironside," and The Old North Church, and we saw the statue epitomizing the famous ride of Paul Revere, I was like a child in a candy store.

My youngest son, Kendrick was a genius when it came to Reading, at age seven, he could pronounce words in the Bible that I could never pronounce. His teacher once told me if he couldn't find anything to read, he would read the dictionary. I was so excited gathering every bit of literature I could put my hands on to bring back for him to read. When we returned home I presented all of this history to him. I just knew he

would pay big money for this. He responded, " I know all about that."
And he never touched it. My feathers fell. Really I was so very proud
of him for his intelligence.

There were so many sights to be seen, and I was enjoying every
moment of it. As I traveled, I never forgot my commitment to God.
Everywhere I went my bible went with me.

I read, and I prayed. I was concerned about one of my boys, William.
He was desiring to make it big in the world in a hurry ,and I was worried
about him. He was full of talent, and was bursting inside to use it.

Once when we had a managers meeting in Springfield, I was assigned
a room alone. I was grateful for this. I could have my time to go to the
Lord, and that I did. I was directed to the book of **Isaiah 54:5-13** his is
His promise and I never forgot it.

Memorial

This year the Stanley Convention was being held in St. Louis. The
Home office had planned a memorial service for Mr. Beverage. They
asked the different officials to search for someone to sing his favorite
song, "In The Garden". My District Manager, Mr. Herbert Lanier,
Quickly responded, "I know someone. " He named me.

When he came to our next sales meeting, he informed us of what
had taken place. He asked me to practice the song for them. I sang it,

and everyone who was not of color announced that they had goose bumps rise upon their skin.

The time drew near for us to depart for St. Louis. When it was time to go to the Airport, it hit me. It had become a reality. I was going to sing onstage before thousands of people. It turned out to be seven thousand, five hundred.

We arrived on Wednesday, and from Wednesday till Friday . My stomach was a ball of butterflies. I couldn't eat anything, my heart was in my stomach. And I had every other feeling that went along with it.

We gathered in the Convention Center, and Stella, and our group sat about two thirds to the front of the Convention Central.

When it was my turn on the program, two of the Stanley officials, from the Home office came up and escorted me onto the stage, all the while encouraging me, "Don't be afraid, Vergie, we're going to be right here beside you."

When I got on the stage, I was more than a little nervous. I looked out over the audience, and all I could see were little dots. I began to sing, the first verse, the Holy Ghost took over and I felt it.

I'll tell you as always, whenever we are at a convention with a crowd that large, and everyone, district by district , zone by zone, giving statistics that no one wants to hear, it would sound like bees buzzing all over the convention center.

It was amazing to me what happened. When I started singing you could hear a pin drop. The sound carried my voice, and every word seemed like an echo. The two officials who were standing by escorted me offstage after I was finished. Stella came running down the aisle to meet me she was so proud of me. She threw her arms around me saying " Vergie, everyone in the audience was crying. "

After the session was over people from all over were running to me asking for my autograph, and they did for years to come. Whenever we would meet, people would ask, "aren't you the one who sang in St. Louis? You sound like Mahalia Jackson." And they would ask me for my autograph. "

God was using me in that way, in that season. After I had played my part and the singing was over I was free as a bird. I was ready to eat , I was ready to tour, I was ready for anything that came my way.

There was one thing I did in St. Louis that I would never do again. I rode up to the top of the Gateway Arch, it was very interesting but very scary. You rode up on a very narrow elevator while seated. When you reached the top, you would get off on a small flat platform, get back on the elevator and ride down the opposite side. From the top you can look over the entire city of St. Louis. But that would be my last time .

During my travels with Stanley Home Products I was introduced to many different dignitaries. Stanley provided many motivational speakers for us. I have lasting memories of most of them, like Zig Ziegler .

The time he spoke at one of our conferences , it was from his book "SEE YOU AT THE TOP "we would have to hold our sides we laughed so hard. But we were motivated when we left. Another speaker was Norman Vincent Peale. Also, the movie actor Bob Hope!!.

On the occasion he spoke to us, I suddenly developed a devastating headache... conveniently ? I found it very very hard to become motivated by his performance.

Lawrence Gets Married

I was now leaving the kids all the time as I moved up the ladder with Stanley. I was the top producer in my zone. I had now become an employee, and was eligible to pay into retirement. I was on my way up the ladder.

Lawrence began to date the oldest daughter of the sister who had died in childbirth. They got married and a year later started a family. The first child was a boy, Corey. And of course, there was the girl Kenya that broke the cycle of boys in the family. The last one was also a boy, Quintrell.

There were many ups and downs in the family. Lawrence was a hard worker, and a good provider for his family. He just recently, shared with me all of the hardships he suffered, because of racism. He went through terrible times on that job. He was always humble and submissive He would have retired with full retirement had he not taken sick before Hurricane Katrina.

Part 4

I LEFT THE CHURCH

Things had gotten so bad at the church that I no longer felt welcome there. I couldn't understand why I was going through what I was going through. I loved the Lord with all my heart, I loved my Pastor and my church family. I was feeling the call of God upon my life. I shared it, and this is when it began.

I felt the strong urge to become a foreign missionary. but I was made to feel ashamed for thinking such thoughts. So, I fell back in my place. While reading the word of God, it was revealed to me that I had put man ahead of God. "God says, thou shall have no other God before me."

This is what I was thinking at the time. Later as I moved on, I started wondering if it was just God's way of getting me to move on. Maybe he was enlarging my territory. When I read the story of how the Apostles were commanded to go into all the world and spread the gospel, they were satisfied to remain right in Jerusalem. **Read MATT 28:19.**

God caused persecution to come upon the church that caused them to scatter and spread the gospel.

It broke my heart. I kept on going to church, only to cry my heart out, and question God, and sit in church, deeply depressed. I was just like a sheep without a shepherd.

I decide to look for another church. I was miserable, and made some very bad decisions. I started visiting a couple of churches looking for the right one. Of course, I was a misfit because of the stance I took for God.

William was no longer attending church. He had met this woman Catherine, that was a few years older than him. He bought a little royal blue pick-up truck. It was at the time of the CB's, where motorists communicated to each other on the road. He would park his truck in the back yard and talk on his CB for hours.

His CB name was "Blue Shoes" and sometimes he was simply called "Blue "especially by his brothers. Most of the time, he talked to "Kat"as she was called. She had a CB set up in home. Before long, he had moved in with her and her family, including her mother. I was devastated. I had thought that my boys and I would be together, in the church, for the rest of our lives. They would get married, have children, and we would all be caught up together with Jesus.

I found out that Kat and her family lived within walking distance from me .I went to have a talk with her mother to no avail. Soon after that they moved into their own apartment.

The owner of the apartment building needed someone to oversee the laundromat so, she asked William and Kat to manage it for her. They moved into the upstairs apartment and lived rent free in exchange for overseeing the laundromat.

Before William had moved out of my home I had gotten the shock of my life. I had begun to notice a change in him. Sleeping more than usual, glossy eyes, and a change in behavior. I searched his room and found a little brown pack of something I had never seen before, way up in the corner of the closet, I knew it was marijuana. My heart sank to my stomach . Not my Child. He had been warned against this very thing he knew how detrimental this could be to his life. I confronted him and pleaded with him in tears.

That was only the beginning of his drug addiction. I thought I had gotten through to him, and that he had moved on with his music. He had bought a base guitar and he and his group would practice music in his back apartment.

This was before he and Kat moved upstairs and he and his group were playing and singing gospel songs. He even got hired by a couple of famous local gospel groups to play base .He had his matching attire, and-that was pretty much all that was required. I soon learned that there were few gospel groups, if any, that didn't use drugs, and alcohol, and chase women. so, he fit right in.

He was not happy ! He wanted to make a lot of money in a hurry. He wanted to produce his own records. He became more and more depressed. He would break out and start crying at times . Once he said to me "if I were white then someone would help me with my music"

I had never seen anyone so utterly depressed. I grieved for him even then. I tried to reach out to him, but he would make sure he would stay out of my way. I could feel the pain that my Son felt and was unable to do anything about it I prayed and solicited the prayers of the saints, but-things got worse.

One night, I had gone to bed and I suddenly got the urge to get up and go to William. It was like a voice speaking to my mind. I knew it was the Lord. I jumped up, threw on a robe and slippers. It was late and raining. I had to go through an alley. there was standing water, so my feet got soaking wet. But that didn't matter. I knocked on the door, William answered. The group was there, rehearsing and smoking Marijuana.

God had revealed to me that there was something else going on. I felt that he was selling drugs. I did not tell him that I thought he was doing that, but that the Lord had shown me what he was doing, and he needed to stop before it was too late. I pleaded with him, and he just looked at me and denied that anything was going on.

I can't remember how long they had lived upstairs before I found out that William was indeed selling drugs. This was my nightmare, come true. I feared for his life every day. Fear consumed me .I would only see William in the street, even though they lived only a few blocks from me, he stayed out of my way. I tried to get close to him, but he would dodge me. The times when I got near him, I would see how depressed and unhappy he was.

He cried a lot. He felt there was no hope for him on this earth. This made me depressed and unhappy. It tore my heart into pieces. I felt so

113

helpless. I had put all my trust in God, and in that hotel room, in Springfield, Massachusetts he had told me that "all my children would be taught of the Lord."

So, I prayed and held on to that promise, and at the same time, I feared for his life because of what he was into just as in the bible Job prayed for his sons and daughters every day, but he was fearful for their lives. **Job: 1:18-19.**

Once he was parked on the corner from my house in his van. Someone had stolen his little blue truck while he was at a grocery store. This just added to his misery.

The truck was eventually found, but he got rid of it and bought this gray van. He was sitting with his feet hanging out of the sliding door. He couldn't run from me this time I hurried to the van before he could move and said to him, "I'm divorcing you." I had heard of children divorcing their parents and vice versa. I was using what some would call reverse psychology I call it wisdom.

It got his attention. His eyes got really big and he repeated, "divorcing me?"

I said, "you don't want to have anything to do with me so that's what I'm doing"

It worked. I was able to establish a relationship with Kat, and they both agreed to attend a Search for Truth Bible Study. Even though William had been raised in the church where we were born again, he had never attended a Bible Study. I had never heard of search for Truth until I became a member of the Apostolic Outreach Center.

I was truly reborn, baptized in Jesus 'name, and full of the Holy Ghost, but when I was offered, and accepted a Bible Study, I discovered there was so much more in the word of God for me.

I would literally come to the edge of my seat as Mike Boyd would teach each lesson. It was so exciting. I could hardly wait for the next week. I was feasting on real "soul food."

I started a Bible Study and it went well for a while, then William started missing. When he was there he would talk about things he had learned from some false doctrine on TV.

He said everyone was destined to die at a certain age, and he would tell us what his age was to die. His mind was messed up from the drugs. He was trying to fill a void that only Jesus could fill. I would tell him this every time I got the chance.

Once he came by and he was high on drugs. I looked him in the face and said, "We have a problem." He looked at me in wide-eyed surprise and said "We"? I said "yes, but we're gonna lick it with the help of Jesus."

I tried reaching him and praying, and requesting prayer for him, but it seemed to no avail. I was told that the drug on the street was "clickum" it made the user click or hallucinate. Once or twice I had witnessed William "clicking." It was horrible. Someone had called me to take him to the hospital. It was like when someone has a mental break down.

I managed to get him in the car, but it was scary. He really needed to be restrained. He didn't know where he was, or who I was. he was all over the car the stirring wheel, and me. It was only by the grace of God we didn't get involved in a serious accident. I managed to get him to Charity Hospital where he was placed on the third floor for the mentally ill. They would keep a patient for three days. I am not sure if they detoxed as well.

William was so naturally smart and intelligent, and had a personality, that everyone admired. So as soon as he came down from his high, or whatever it was, he was entertaining the staff and was soon out of there.

One day I got a call from him. He had been riding in the car with someone and they got stopped by the police and they found drugs in the car. They all went to jail. I was overjoyed. God had answered my prayers. I immediately contacted the Prison Ministry from church.

They were ready to go to work. My prodigal son was coming home. I can't remember if it was late that night, or the next morning, I answered a knock at the door and there stood William. I was shocked, disappointed, and angry at the law. How could they let him out? Didn't they know he was gonna self-destruct? It had been a false arrest or a violation of their rights or something. They had been pulled over illegally and they had to let them go.

My faith was not strong at all. At the least, it was wavering . It was up and down. I was in turmoil. I kept teaching Bible study to Katherine. William would either show up late, or leave when I got there, but he was now stopping by and we would talk. Things began to get ugly between William and Kat. She would call me and tell me how he was physically abusing her. She was calling the cops almost every day on him.

I always felt that what my boys did was a reflection on me. Everyone would think I was an unfit Mother because my children had gone astray. I couldn't sleep . I was in a very bad place. And I feared for his life, and worried about what people thought of me. Finally, the fighting got so bad between the two of them, they got kicked out of the apartment.

There was a big fight and the two of them were arrested. I was delighted to see him go to jail. Now he could get help. The Prison Ministry from the Church would be anxious to minister to him and he would come back to God. Her folks got her out , and she got him out.

Surely this was the plan of Satan. They could not go back to the apartment, she went to live with a sister, and he found a room down the street from Sis Watson. It seemed that God had finally answered my prayers.

He got a job as a sitter. He called me every day and poured out his heart to me. He would stop by to see me but wouldn't stay very long I later found out the reason for that. He looked so handsome in his white uniform. He was the tallest of my Sons, and had my complexion, and my features.

In My Pursuit of a Church

In my pursuit of church that I could call home, I started attending a church in Baker, Louisiana. One of my Stanley hostesses and her family had become my friends, and they had become dissatisfied with some wrongdoing that was going on in the church, where her brother was the Pastor.

The church in Baker was pastored by one of her two sons, called the Bishop. The youngest one was called the Prophet. There was a promise that the Prophet would start a church in New Orleans, as soon as we could find some property.

We were excited, and looking forward to the coming event. We would drive there every Sunday, waiting for him to find property.

The Bishop was preaching the truth as he knew it. He did not have the revelation of the oneness as yet, but he was sincere, and preached and taught against sin. There were no Holiness standards, but I was so hungry for the word and the fellowship. I kept going, but stood my ground and upheld my standards.

I refused to conform!

Well, the opportunity came to start their church in New Orleans,. When the A&P grocery store closed down, right down the street from me, on St. Claud Avenue they purchased the building. They set up a tent to hold services while waiting for the building to be renovated.

The Prophet had posted some of the young men to guard the tent at night, since it contained all of the church equipment. One night the police busted them smoking weed under the tent. That was the end of that activity.

So, the Church began, and it was a nightmare.

Just before the building was finished in New Orleans, William had accepted my invitation to come to church with me. He was recruited to play his guitar. To me William was on his way back to the Lord. We went on events and he brought his bass guitar. He would play that bass, and every eye would be on him.

Every service there would be a "prophecy line." Whatever size offering you gave, that was the size prophesy you received. As far as myself, I became an outcast. Every type of sin was welcomed there.

When we went to event we carpooled. I rode with some of the ladies. I would get sick from inhaling cigarette smoke. When I let my window down to get some air, I was rebuked. ""Ain't nobody that holy" they would say. I was asked, " why don't you wear pants. And I explained. They ran to the Prophet to tell him the news, rather to report me.

The next service I was rebuked from the pulpit. It's just a " little piece of pants" he said. A picnic was planned for the church, and he had encouraged the women to wear bathing suits. When I refused to conform, he called a meeting with me to convert me to **UNHOLINESS**. I have never been disrespectful, disobedient or disloyal to any authority. However, I stood my ground, and held to what I knew to be the truth of God's word. That did not set well at all.

One afternoon when I went to the church. It was now finished, and we were in the building. To my surprise, one of the girls who had been smoking in the car, physically attacked me for no reason at all. I was shocked.

I went to my friend, the prophets Mother in tears. To. my dismay, she took the defense of the other girl. I was foolish enough to go to the prophet with my woes against his mother. Of course. He took his mother's side.

I was trapped. I had been missing some of the services, but I couldn't just stay home. I had to go to church. I was in despair. This was such a lonely place to be.

"Help Lord!!"

William's Trials Continue

After the physical attack, I stayed home as much as I could. I was trying to encourage William and be there for him. I had never heard more beautiful stringed music. It was heavenly. He had a desire to play only for God. If his music was not pleasing to God, he was willing to change it. My heart was so full of gratitude to God. He had heard my cry , and answer my prayers. He had mercy on my son. He had listened

120

to my plea. Those days all my focus was on William, and getting him back to God. I was not even a part of the congregation any more I was being shunned, even by my friend, the Prophet's mother.

I thought I could have made a difference, a light in darkness. I don't know why I stayed there so long. Things happened there that should have sent me running.

As I look back now I think, it must have been "GOD'S PERFECT PLAN " for my life.

The Invitation

It was right at this time that some friends of mine, Kenneth and Ethel came to me with some information. I had met Ethel through Stanley Home Products, as a Hostess and they were having similar problems at their church such as myself.

Ethel's cousin was the pastor of the church where they were members. He was living in adultery, and they were filled with the Holy Ghost filled. His behavior was unacceptable to them.

They came to me and told me they were having a Bible study with a sister from an Apostolic Church, I was skeptical having met some Apostolic's as they were different from us.

One lady was a friend of Sis Banks. She wore heavy brogan shoes, thick white stockings, black skirts to the ankles and sleeves to the wrist, at all times. They were not allowed to straighten their hair. I didn't think that was what I was looking for.

The next week they came back to me telling me about another lesson they were being taught on the Tabernacle plan. I knew I didn't want to get involved in that.

That was Spiritualism. I knew of a church back of town that practiced that. One day one of my dealers and I were knocking on doors booking parties. When the lady opened the door we could see other ladies inside dancing around lit candles and calling up the dead. We got out of there faster than fast. Nope, didn't want to go near anything like that.

But I soon learned that I was wrong. They kept after me, and I thank God to this day that they did. All that persecution, all the hurt, the disappointment was not for naught.

The master potter was putting me through the fire. He was molding me, shaping me He was preparing me for such a time as this. He wanted to bring me to *"Higher Heights"* in Him.

Yes, this was His "Perfect Plan."

Kendrick Goes to the Navy

At this time, I had moved into a home that my sister Betty and her husband Marvin had bought on the corner of Renee, and St. Claude. They had upgraded to another house in New Orleans East. I had taken over the notes on this one. It was just before Lawrence got married. He and Tricia had eventually followed me to the Church on St Claude and were still attending.

After William moved out it was Kendrick and me. He had decided to join the Navy and completed his boot camp. He decided not to make a career out of the military and was honorably discharged.

When he would relay to me how disciplined he had to be, that made me the happiest . He had to fold towels to look like a razor's edge. He had to spit clean his shoes, and all of his surroundings had to be immaculate.

Oh, happy day!! At least when he came back, I wouldn't have to worry about him keeping his room clean. Was I in for a big disappointment. As soon as he put his foot in the door upon his return, I was introduced to the junkyard once again.

My New Home

I accepted the invitation to go to the Apostolic Outreach Center with Kenneth and Ethel. But I kept both my eyes open. I was not going to jump out of the frying pan into the fire. Was I mistaken. When I walked into the building I saw beautifully, yet modestly dressed Saints of God.

When Pastor Brown got up to preach, I observed he was preaching the same gospel that I knew to be the word of God. I went back the second Sunday and by that time I was sold. I decided that I would make this my new home. Singing had always been my second love and when I heard the Choir sing, I thought, " I will be satisfied just to stand on the back row and sing be a back-up singer. I went to the choir director and asked what I had to do to become a part of that beautiful choir. He in turn told me to talk to the Pastor Brown which I did.

He asked, " Have you been baptized in Jesus name, and received the Holy Ghost ?"

Of course, my answer was yes! Then I thought of what I had heard from certain denominations, that "God didn't call no woman to preach." Even though I knew what I had received was real, and had come from God. God had used a vessel, no gender, to perform this miraculous work in me, and no one could take it away. But if God had more light for me, I was going to walk in it. So, I added, I've been baptized , but it was by a woman. He looked at me and said, "They're good people." Okay!!! I was on my way, up to higher heights, in Him.

The Struggle

William was striving to get back to God, but there was a force that was stronger than him that was holding him back. I assured him that God saw his struggle and that together we could take it to Him. We wrestled with the enemy. I would have given up anything to see my son delivered from this hell.

I had seen the war going on inside of him for so long. He was tormented beyond measure. And I was fighting for his life. One day after he had moved out, when I was cleaning his room, I had found some writings that he had written. They were demonic, horrible, scenes and graphics, and words, not in any eearthly language .straight from the pits of hell. Words that only Satan could understand. But they were coming from the mind of my son.

I knew they came from Satan. I had never seen anything so evil coming from a human being. This was more than I could bear. I had no answers to what was happening to him. I was devasted, my heart was broken. I was powerless to help him. I felt every pain, every burden, the depression he suffered, I also suffered.

Every opportunity I got, I poured out my love into him. He knew I loved him. .He knew that his problem was my problem. And I let him know that every single time we were together. I would never desert him, and he knew it.

He was unstable, and restless, but finally the tide began to turn. He became stable and got another job as a sitter. He wanted so badly to turn his life around and turn it over to God again. So, he wanted to work to make an honest living. I was so proud of him. He looked so tall and so handsome in his white uniform.

Now he was making his way back to God. He would call me from the hospital and talk ,expressing his feelings to me. "Kat keeps pressuring me to marry her, but she can't have any children and I want children."

I would stay on the phone for hours with him while his patient slept. He would say, "Mama, I'm so depressed" I listened to him, cried with him, and encouraged him. He would tell me, "Mama, I'm sitting here looking out the window." Then he would describe what it was he saw. The things he saw and described were through the eyes of God. He would call me from his apartment every Sunday morning, and tell me, "Mama, I'm sitting here listening to Jimmy Swaggart."

God was working on him. He wanted to get away from his old life. He told me, "Mama, I'm trying to get away from them, but they keep following me." The people he was talking about were the ones he had sold drugs to.

He knew God loved him. He knew I loved him. He knew that his problem was my problem. I let him know that together, we could take it to God. We wrestled with the enemy. Now he was making his way back to God.

Kendrick Runs Away

I was still working for Stanley Home Products having less home demonstration, but I could get on the phone and sell a thousand dollars' worth, of products on any given weekend.

Kendrick was the only one left at home to help me bag and deliver. And he got his share of pay one way or the other. He had become restless and somewhat defiant.

He began dating a girl named Stephanie who lived two houses from us before we moved. Now we were living right around the corner. Stephanie was a sweet girl and I already loved her like a daughter.

One Friday night I kind of pressured Kendrick into helping me bag orders for delivery. He had shown his displeasure in doing so. I went into the other room and when I came back Kendrick was gone along with the money that had been collected previously.

When I couldn't find him , I was devasted. That night turned into two months that I didn't hear from Kendrick. I died a thousand deaths. I couldn't eat, I couldn't sleep. This had been the first time either one of my boys had been out of my sight, that I didn't know where they were. I grieved over him every day.

Stephanie's mother, upon my request, allowed her to come every night to sleep over with me, because I couldn't bear to be alone. Having her near me was somewhat like having him home. She was maybe fourteen at the time, but she was so kind, and caring, and understanding. She was grieving for him also, and we were a comfort to one another.

I put out a missing report on him, and I was calling the detective every day. He didn't mine at all. I was persistent but I was kind. He went the extra mile, he told me, because of my attitude. I was just a desperate mother, longing to find her son. I prayed, I cried, and begged God to send him back.

I heard of this so called prophet who could prophesy as to the whereabouts of missing love ones. He turned out to be fraud just out for money. The minute I saw him, God said no!

I was so helpless. I imagined him lying dead in ditch. All sorts of horrible things had happened to him. Stephanie and I went through this together, leaning on each other. I went through hell on earth.

Then finally one day I received a postcard from him. It was from somewhere in Texas. He was ready to let me know where he was. Or rather he had decided he had punished me long enough, and was ready to come home. He had been working for a temporary agency getting paid by the day and had been living in a hotel. Stephanie and I both were overjoyed.

By the time I could try to track him down at the Hotel, he had caught the bus, and was on his way home. He did a lot of that kind of activity in the times to come. He wanted to live a hippie life. He later told me he was hopping freight trains as his means of travel. I never knew exactly what it was he was going through.

During one period when he was semi-settled, he and William shared an apartment together. It was above a grocery store that I was managing for the owner, Ernie. That is when he met Shemel. She became pregnant He informed me of his intentions to marry her However she became so aggressive toward him, she literally drove him away. He stayed his course during the pregnancy , but they did not marry.

After nine months, the most precious gift was born. Terry was to become a prevalent part of my life.

Passing of Sister Banks

In 1983, Sister Banks took sick. She would call me often and ask different things of me .I would check on her, and go to see her, but it seemed as if she was trying to make up for the time we had been apart. My sister Betty told me that there were some things that she regretted. She would tell me" I want you to come and sing for me" and told me I had music in my voice.

Of course, I was willing to fill her every request. She would ask me to cook her some greens, and I did. In the meantime, my sister Betty, and Iola were serving as caregivers for her. One night after I had visited her and went home, my sister called me and told me Sis Banks was asking for me.

I hurried back to her house, which was about a mile. When I got there she called me to the bed. This was the message she had for me. " Verge, I'm tired, I'm going home to be with Jesus. I want you to play the piano at my funeral." That was the hardest request to agree to fill for her. She had come from the Church of God In Christ (COGIC). That is where her funeral was held, and I honored her request and played the piano, and sang for her.

I was a member of Apostolic Outreach Center, but I would visit the church that Sister Banks had pastored, and where I had been born again. My sister and her family were still attending . After attending AOC for a month, Pastor Green, passed away suddenly.

He died on a Saturday night, and the shocking news spread rapidly by that Sunday morning. His memorial service was held that Sunday night, at the First Pentecostal. Church. All of the surrounding churches closed their night service to attend his Memorial.   One of the young men that had become a part of Sister Banks congregation had just taken over, with no direction from God nor man. He was spewing out all kinds of heresy from the pulpit. There was utter chaos in the church. The people were like scattered sheep. They didn't know what to do or where to go.

As I observed the situation ,as always by the leading of the Lord, I came to the rescue. Pastor John Cupit, with the First Pentecostal Church on Canal Street had become pastor of the AOC congregation after the passing of Pastor Green.

I went to him and relayed the situation. He sent different ministers in training from AOC to conduct the services, with the intenttion that the people would choose one of them to become their permanent pastor. The last one to go as a fill in was Brother Larry Haynes. He and his wife

Peggy became permanent pastors, and are still pastoring a church today in Slidell, Louisiana.

The Haynes and I were close friends since I had become a member of the AOC. We had some wonderful times of fellowship together. There was the need for a musician, so I was asked to help out..

I directed both an adult, and children choir. Their oldest daughter, Chanel , had a very powerful ,anointed voice, and as a little girl was a part of that choir, she later became a worldwide gospel singer. I'm sure God ordained her from her mother's womb to bless the world with her anointing.   She and two others girls formed a group and named it, " Trinity 5:7, according to 1 John 5:7. I can't believe that every time we have had the privilege to run into each other, she tells me I'm her favorite gospel singer. I'm sure she is only being kind..

Kendrick Meets Destiny

During the time I was helping out with the music on Egania Street I met this young lady at AOC, who had come from New York. She was living with a church family along with her eleven year old daughter.

I befriended everyone I met, so we communicated at church . She was originally from another country and became upset with the leadership over something of her own doing. She asked to come to the morning service with me, at the other cchurch one Sunday. I was happy to accommodate her.

It was at the same time that Kendrick had moved back in with me. He had a very good paying job working at Barry's warehouse. His apartment was in a not so suitable nneighborhood. One night there was police raid and he made it all the way to my house on foot, huffing and puffing. It was somewhat funny.

Every child, no matter how tough they appear to be, knows how to find Mama in ttimes of distress. Well, I was delighted for him to come in for a while. This was my opportunity to get him back to God. One of the stipulations was that he go to church at least on Sunday. He was fine with that.

I picked Destiny up and we went to the morning service. When we picked her up, she and Kendrick began eyeing each other. Kendrick got Baptized after service. I had found out earlier that he had gotten involved with smoking marijuana.

He and his brothers were very close, and it seemed they both looked up to William even though Lawrence was the oldest. William was a born leader. Well, Kendrick followed pursuit after his big brother.

He became convicted from the message and was baptized again that day. We went out for Chinese food after church and I could sense that something unpleasant was about to take place.

We dropped Destiny off and went home. Within an hour, she was at my house via bicycle. I was so outdone.

She was six years older than Kendrick, but that was not the problem. Kendrick had begun his way back to the Lord. She pursued him every day that week by riding her bike to the house. I knew this was the trick of the enemy to bring a distraction to what God was doing in Kendrick's life.

I invited her out to lunch for a heart to heart talk with her to try and explain why it was so important to leave him alone for now. I explained to her that he needed to focus on getting his life right with God.

She responded in her native accent, " He half saved." Meaning he was half saved because he got baptized, maybe not realizing there were three steps to salvation. That day, I became her worse enemy.

Kendrick was just trying to make a comeback to God and was very fragile. I was aware that something she had shared with me would be detrimental to his returning to God. I tried to warn him of the danger, and he repeated it to her.

She called me that very afternoon, gave me a good cussing out while I held the phone, not saying a word. She informed me that she would "Morry him or shock up with him." Weeks later they went to the courthouse, and got married.

William Prophesied His Own Death

William had left his little apartment, which was located on the back side of town, because he was determined to get away from his old environment. I invited him to move in with me. This was the perfect opportunity to be close to him , counsel with him and pray with him. He moved all his belongings into the house, but he would not sleep inside. This was puzzling to me. I later learned the reason behind this. There was a rash of murders in New Orleans. If some one had a grudge against someone ,or if a family member had been killed, a member of that family retaliated against a member of their family.

So, William slept in his van which he parked across the street from my house. This was his way of protecting me. He would come inside, take a bath and shave and go his way.

I never slept. I would go across the street every so often to see if he was in the van. My heart stayed in my stomach. I imagined the worst. I was a wreck, until finally, I would peak through the rear window of the van and there he was, fast asleep. Then I would go inside and try to get some sleep.

He never knew I was checking on him . I was never at ease when I didn't know where he was. He had a lot of ups and downs There were times when he would spend time with the family, and he could hold your attention with the most interesting conversations.

He was so gifted, so special. I had no doubt that God was dealing with him.

One time when he was trying to blend with the family, we were at my sister Betty's house. He had everyone's attention. He was telling us about pass events that we were not aware of, and things that he desired. His dreams.

He told us of the time he almost drowned in a pool at a recreation center. He was still a child, or maybe a teenager. I had sent them to camp that summer. And there was one thing that he talked about that day, that I tried to un-hear.

He was talking about this doctrine he had heard on TV, that predicted the age that everyone would die. He said of himself, " Of course I'll probably die some kind of weird death.." He had prophesied his death.

Now the church on Egania Street had a musician and I was helping out at the First Church, with Johnathan Cupit with worship service . By now, Lawrence and his family were attending AOC .

One night we had an Evangelist at church. I invited him to come. He was getting off work early, now that he had a daytime position. He was so anxious to come. He came straight from work in his white uniform. I couldn't have been more proud.

He sat near the back. I sat with him, but had to go up and help with the Worship Service. At this time, I was playing piano, and learning to play the Organ.   Our previous musician had moved away. There were long preliminaries everything was happening except the word. One thing after the other went on, but no word.

I was sitting waiting for my opportunity to go and sit with him. All of a sudden he jumped and left out of the door. I had felt the same thing he was feeling. He's hungry for the Word. To me, it seemed this revival service should be all about him and the other desperate souls who had come to get something from God. Someone was dropping the ball. Was God getting the glory? was I being selfish, and judgmental?

I got up and followed him. He was in the parking lot fighting with a flat tire on his gray van. This only added to his frustration. My heart went out to him. Satan didn't want to let him go. I tried to convince him to come back inside and wait until service was over. But he was determined to get away.

His emotions were all over the place. He had to go to work the next morning and it was already late. He told me then that he had come to hear the Word, but they were doing everything else but preaching.

I went inside and got one or two brothers to come out and help him with his tire. Who knows. Maybe his tire went flat for a reason. Maybe God was putting him to the test. We can never understand the ways of God.

One of the guests that night was Gerald Joseph. His wife, Bridget had experienced something similar to what William was going through. I watched God bring her back from the pits of hell. She had OD'ed more than once, according to her testimony. and was suicidal. She would rock back and forth, and looked the part of someone struggling with addiction. I watched as God delivered her and brought her back to the beautiful Woman of God she is today on fire for Him and preaching His Word,.

Gerald got filled with the Holy Ghost. I didn't understand why things didn't turn out differently that night? Why didn't William get what he came for?

As Pastor Cupid often said to me when I was going through, we can't track God, but can trust Him. "His judgements are unsearchable, and His ways are past finding out." **Romans 11:33** .

The devil was pulling as hard as he could to keep William away from God. Every time he made the effort to get back, there was some force holding him back, but I kept praying for him and loving him.

I didn't give up on inviting him to church every time I got the chance. Since he had gotten disappointed with the service at AOC. I decided to invite him to First Church. The regular services at the First Church were held at ten o'clock , and three o'clock at AOC.

I invited William to the First Church. He met me there, and I was overjoyed. To see him sitting on that pew was the most beautiful sight I had ever seen.

He went with me to the afternoon service that Sunday. At the Altar service, I was singing my heart out ,with my eyes closed. All of a sudden

I heard Pastor call my name, rather loudly, " Sis Vergie, your boy is over there speaking in tongues". I literally dropped the mike and ran to the other side.

He was re-baptized that day. God had given him another chance. He had come home. After service, we talked to Pastor Cupit, and he set up a Church for Truth Bible study for William with Brother Richard Dykes.

Brother Dykes started the study at my home. In the meantime, William would work on his songs, in hopes of getting a break someday soon. He would play my piano, then the drums, plus his bass guitar, which he cherished. I was one of the backup singer's. He had written several songs. One among them was "Jesus Christ, Super Star"

Everybody has a hero,

So many People have someone

they'd like to be.

I wanna tell you about my hero,

He means all the world to me,

Jesus Christ, He's my Super Star.

When the sitting jobs were slow, He would pick up jobs as a waiter through a Temp Service. During one of these periods, The Church held our Christmas Banquet at the hotel where he was working. He happened to be our waiter. He looked so handsome in his waiters uniform. His tall lean form somehow made him fit the role as a waiter. He had slightly curly hair with a patch of larger curls at the base of his neck. When he smiled, he would light up the room. He had big dreams. He loved music

You could never imagine in a thousand years what a proud mother I was. When he was born, for some reason I called him my "Blue Baby" He was the only one that had my dark complexion, as well as my features.

The Bible study continued, but Brother Dykes had turned it over to Brother Julius Ford, since he had to fill some other commitment. He was engrossed in the word. He listened intently. He asked questions and humbly received instructions.

He had spoken to our Choir Director, Brother Thaddeus about playing for the music department and he was going to put him to work. He was concerned about whether his music was too worldly. He asked Brother Ford's advice. I don't know what he told him, but he was willing to do whatever it took to please " his hero".

Williams Birthday

Tuesday September, 10, was Williams birthday. He had gone fishing on the riverbanks.. He caught a few fish and brought them home to cook .He was determined to share them with me. It was so good I asked for more. He pushed the last potion over and said "Here, take it all." This was one of my fondest memories I have of him, and also one of the saddest, because he was willing to deny himself for me.

On Thursday he was riding in a car with some other guys. Right at the corner of our street someone ran into them. He came inside and got a broom so he could sweep the glass up saying, to me, "Mama, everybody says that Friday the 13th is bad luck, but it's gonna be a good day for me."

How could he know? There could not have been a truer statement. For him, it was to be a very good day. Not so much for me as he would be going home on Friday to his new heavenly home.

To reflect back some of my family didn't see him as God saw him. I was there when he made his way back to God. When he spoke in tongues, and got re-baptized that Sunday.

When Pastor Cupit got my attention, as I stood singing and praying at the same time as they prayed with him. They hadn't spent hours on end with him late nights as we talked about the things of God. How he would look out the hospital window as he sat with his patients, and tell me things that were magical. How he would call me on Sunday morning and express his plans to serve in the kingdom of God.

But "God had another plan, A PERFECT PLAN"

Yes! He was judged by some, and condemned by others.

That Day

Stella and I had gone to Houma, Louisiana, to promote Kayak swimming pools in the Mall. She had taken a break from Stanley Home

Products, but I was still servicing my customers, ordering and delivering their products. I had put some products in my car to deliver to a customer back of town that afternoon.

On my way back home, I met William walking down the street he was excited because he had applied for a new waiter's position and had gotten hired. The day before after sweeping the glass off the street, from the little car accident, he had come inside to get his uniform ready. I can picture him now ,eager to check it out to make sure it was in order.

I had gotten up that morning and cooked cabbage with him in mind. He was always in my mind. He had come a long way, but he still had a long way to go. The drugs had played havoc on his mind, but there was a gentleness about him. I knew God was dealing with him, and had plans for him. How could I know that He was getting him ready to bring him home? He seemed to have developed this special love for me. I had never scolded him for his problems, just loved him and prayed for him.

We would pray together, and we shared a special bond. I believe he would have given his life for me. In these last months he was protecting me when he refused to sleep in the house, but slept in his van. He had shared so many of his thoughts and dreams with me. I was so happy to see him. I stopped and told him I had cooked cabbage for him, and asked if he had gone inside to eat .He said no, but he would be home in a little while and eat.

141

I went home and preceded to get some Stanley orders ready to send off. All the time I was anxiously waiting for him to come home. I looked forward to our chats and listening to him pour out his heart.

My mind would wonder back to the times when he would walk the streets, head bowed down, shoulders humped, crying, believing he had no hope .He felt he had no one to turn to, to talk to. He was running from God, the only one that could help him .And he ran from me , the one who would lead him back to God.

'That Day,' I told him I was divorcing him was the turning point. that got his attention. Since then he knew how much I loved, and cared about him. He could talk to me about anything and I would listen. Nothing shocked me, he knew I would not criticize, judge or condemn him. And he knew that there was nothing too hard for God to take care of.

The phone rang. It was Kat. Someone had called her and told her "Blue" had gotten shot. I can't remember what I felt at that moment. I kept on doing what I was doing. Maybe that's when I went numb.

Ethel White my friend who had introduced me to AOC, was staying with me temporarily. There had been a Hurricane ,and her home had been severely damaged .She had contracted some preacher to repair her home, payed him up front, he had taken her money and was nowhere to be found She could not live in her house, the roof was off.

She called me heartbroken, and I told her, come on over. She and her daughter Kim came to live with me until she could get on her feet.

I sat there and went about my business, refusing to believe there was any truth to that phone call. I called my friend Sister Lillie Knight to tell her the rumor. She said, "I don't believe that." Just what I wanted to hear

I went back to getting my orders together. When Ethel came home from work a short time later, I casually mentioned it to her She said, "I'm going and see." Cat had told me where it had supposedly happened.

When Ethel returned, she told me that it was true. She said that they had him in the ambulance working on him, desperately trying to save his life. There was one of his blue slip-on tennis shoes in the street, and that's how she knew it was him.

I called Lawrence, my oldest, he in turn called his Brother Kendrick. They picked up Pastor Cupit and they went to the morgue. When they returned Lawrence came in and fell on my neck. Pastor Cupit didn't have the words to express his sorrow.

This was the end of my World.

Grief sets in

In the days that followed I was just numb. I didn't feel much of anything . I had heard talk of people grieving the death of a loved one before they died. Surly that is what I had done.

I didn't know about the different stages of grief at that time. I would tell everyone who came around that God had prepared me for this. In the days that followed I later learned from reading articles on grief that this is God's way of cushioning the shock. I had heard of people dropping dead after learning of the sudden death of a loved one.

I will go into details of the different stages of grief later in the book. The one time I broke down was when a friend came to pick up something for the funeral home for William. His name was Robert, and he played bass at the church . He and William would have been playing interchangeable, if William had lived. When Robert came, and I had to go get the items that he needed, reality set in. It hit me that William was really gone.   Death is so final.

Robert was the only one to see me cry before the funeral, " I had begun to feel." It was as if my heart had been ripped out and left this big raw putrefying hole in its place.

My family began to arrive from out of town As people gathered around me, I went into numbness mode again. All of my relatives from out of town had gone to sleep at my son Lawrence's house. My oldest sister, who was on dialysis, had defied her doctor to come and be with me. She was the only one to sleep at my house. What was wrong with everybody? I was the one who needed them.

How could they be so insensitive? They were running from me. This was just the beginning of people running from me. Yet I hid my feelings. My sister sensed what I was feeling, and tried to comfort me.   The next time I broke down was at the end of the service when it was time for the viewing. I heard my sister Betty, who had not seen me cry before now say, "She is starting to grieve." I realized that this would be the last time I would see my precious son. I wanted to touch him one last time, but someone held me back. This is one of the memories etched in my mind to this day. I was crying, "Don't hold me back!"

But they would not let me go. In time of loss and grief, people will say or do what they think is helpful, but it has the opposite effect, even though their intentions are good. I felt like I had been robbed of those last moments with my baby.

Part 4

After the Funeral

The funeral was over, and everybody had gone home. I was almost alone. But there was Terry, the baby boy that was born almost two years before William died.

I had already fell in love with him. I don't know the words to describe what it was with Terry I have always had a heart for children. .Not just my own. After Williams death, the bond between us was so strong, nothing would ever be able to break it . William had fallen in love with him also. He loved his uncle William.

One day when he hadn't seen him for a while , as I was holding him in my arms, he looked up at me and asked," Where is Uncle William?" I answered sadly, "Baby, Uncle. William is dead ".

He answered back, "He not dead!" Oh! If he only knew how I wished he could just speak it and it would be true.

I know that I was trying to replace that awful deep, raw ,rotten place in my heart. I clung to him for dear life. There was no one else that I could keep that close to me. He wouldn't run from me. I have left out some awful details concerning situations involving Terry and me because of my intention to telling my story is to build up, and not tear down any one.   I will mention one incident here, and others throughout this story. Kendrick had been forbidden to see his son ever since he got

147

married. I was instrumental in helping them to rent their own apartment right across the street from me.

I would have done just about anything to have someone near me, to go through this with me. But Kendrick was not permitted to come across the street. I would bring Terry to my home every day. William would be the one to get him before he died.

Kendrick came over to see him one day, and Destiny came to me and made a request, or a command?. She said, in her native accent, Vergie! I don't want that child at your house cause Kendrick will be coming over here to see him."

At that moment, I was shocked, I was torn, I was hurt, I was grieving. It surprised me what I answered her. I said " okay, I won't bring him back over here. This was my house, but I had agreed not to bring this innocent little child here for fear his father would see him. How cruel!

She had told me once that Pastor Green had said ,"Don't bring them outside children into your "Morrage." However, she had an eleven year old and had never been married. I must not keep this part out, in order to show how heartless and cruel people can be.

Oh! the terrible decisions you can make when you're grieving. What was wrong with me? She was the one that was totally crazy. There was no way I was going to desert my baby, my pillar, my one and only comfort for her selfish desires. He had begun to feel the rejection of his father, and he needed me as much as I needed him. So, I ignored her, and kept on doing what I had been doing, bonding and loving this precious, innocent little boy.

A Child in Despair

I had taken Terry into my bosom. He was my grandson and I took him with me everywhere I went for at least fifteen years.

When I went on vacation, he went with me. Our church choir traveled all over from Louisiana, Washington, Texas, and other states. After he was old enough to travel he traveled with me. Whenever we went on an event a seat on the tour bus was always reserved for him.

This child meant the world to me. I took him as my own. I bought his clothes, his school supplies, his toys, and I was the one to attend his school functions and visit his teachers. The teachers were amazed, and often expressed their amazement over the fact that someone would do these things for a child that was not their own. But I had made him my own. He had been abandoned by his father and his Mother felt comfortable with me taking care of him. In those times of grieving I would have been worst off if I hadn't had him in my life.

It was a sad ,sad time in his life. My heart broke for him. He longed for his father. He would tell me his desires, but they have never been fulfilled. "I wanna go fishing with my Daddy," I just wanna spend one night in my Daddy's House"

Even though we were in walking distance of each other, it never happened. Try as I may, I could not comfort him concerning his dad. I never spoke against his dad, but always built him up in his eyes.

I always told him his dad loved him ,but was having some problems that prevented him from being with him right now. I would buy his birthday and Christmas gifts in the name of his dad. But nothing or no one can ever take the place of a mother, or a father in the heart of a child. Many, many times we would ride in the car and play little games. We would see which one of us could outdo the other, with name calling. It had to be the names of animals. We would go from an ant to a hippopotamus , and we would laugh till we cried.

Those were our happy moments.

But there were always some sad moments with the both of us. I signed him up for baseball and I was the only one to go to his games. I remember one day I was having symptoms of a heart attack, so, I drove myself to Methodist Hospital.

Terry had a game the following night but after the doctor examining me, he informed me that they would have to admit me to do an angiogram. And I informed them that I couldn't be admitted, because my baby had a ballgame the following evening.

They promised to call the right person and let them know the situation. Somehow my son Lawrence got the news and rushed to the hospital in a panic. "Ma, what's wrong". They had the little air tubes in my nose, and he had never seen me in that position. He has always been protective of me.

Well, they did the angiogram ,discharged me the next afternoon, and I made my way straight from the hospital, to the park. Weak as water. I can't remember who got him to the park. I will never understand how any parent can desert an innocent little child, How can one be so selfish, and cruel, to ignore the cry of a little child just to be loved by its mother or father. To be rejected, or abandoned will effect an individual for the rest of their lives, except for the healing power of God.

This precious little boy went to Vacation Bible school every summer, and wanted to at least be excepted by other members of the family but was rejected by them also.

One day after the class I went home and didn't stay for the activities. He came running home so crushed, because several children had been invited to go to the home of his relatives, but he was told he couldn't come. He just couldn't win for losing.

My heart would bleed for him. It was just Terry and I couldn't do anything to make the hurt go away, and it broke my heart.

The second most painful thing to grieving over the death of my son, was my going through with this precious child's, longing, hurting, crying, and agonizing over the rejection of a loved one and family.

I don't know why. But God chose me, and placed them in my care, for a season. I am committed to do his will.

Vergie Iglus

Kendrick's Dark Journey

After the death of his brother, Kendrick was having a hard time coping. He would stand in the doorway on cold days and ask his wife if she thought William was cold out there in the graveyard. We eventually had to get some professional help for him. He was in a real vulnerable state. However, there seemed to be no helping him. It was so sad hearing about what he was going through. This just added to my grief.

Pastor Vernon Brite from Macon, Georgia, had come to minister at our church and Kendrick's wife felt that if she could get Kendrick away from the environment he would do better.

Macon, Georgia, seemed like a good place to go since there was a good church there.

William had backed his van in the driveway on the side of the house before he was killed. I had not seen the rear of it since it was parked there. Kendrick had taken it over, and when he drove it out that's when I saw the placard that he had scribbled on. He had named his beloved van , 'Little Vergie."

It brought a moment of peace to me. I was so grateful that I had reached out to him. I had fought for him, I had stood with him, I had not given up on him. I had loved him unconditionally and he had felt my love. That warmed my heart. I wish that I could have held on to that placard as a reminder of the bond we shared.

152

So, Kendrick along with Destiny and Trudy set out for Macon in the van named 'Little Vergie.

There are many stages of Grief

There are many articles written on grief, etc. However, everyone grieves differently. In this book, I will be revealing firsthand, my grieving experience.

Prayerfully, hopefully, someone who has found themselves in the same state will know that there is a way out of the deep dark pit of despair.

As I stated previously, when my son's death was confirmed, I went numb. I felt God had prepared me for this so after every one went home, I began to feel the loss, the finality of his death. I found it very hard to keep up my routine of working with Stanley.

Nothing had any meaning anymore. I remember one night I was going to deliver some products to my customer on my way to church. I had to pass the bus stop where my son had been shot. It was as if I had just witnessed the scene taking place. By the time I arrived at the lady's home, I was hysterical. I couldn't talk, and she had no idea what was going on with me.

I finally regained my composure and explained the situation. From then on, I had to go miles out of the way to avoid passing that spot. I finally gave up my position as manager with Stanley Home Products.

Stella kept me busy doing different jobs, for which I was grateful. We continued promoting kayak swimming pools in various malls. Once we had a job exchanging greeting cards in different pharmacies. I would work myself into a stupor. I could hardly make it inside my house. I managed to get a bath and if I couldn't fall asleep right away I would call one of the two people who would listen to me, who didn't run away from me.

I didn't know what I was saying. I just rattled on for hours on end. Talking about William. Once during a conversation with Raymond one of my listeners, he said to me, "Sister Vergie, William is gone now, you need to let go.

"That was like a stab in my heart. I was finished talking to him. He didn't understand. He had not lost a child; he didn't even have a child. Of course, I resumed my talks with him, but I held back some of my feelings.

I just needed someone to talk to. The other person was sweet Sister Lodge , my friend, and Sister in the Lord. She would listen, to me, never tiring, until I would fall asleep. During my grieving period she became ill, and God called her home.

I was in a very fragile state of mind. My heart just couldn't seem to be able to handle the misery that I was going through In fact I had no heart left . My heart had been ripped out and in its place was this hole that was raw, and infectious.

I just wanted to go and be with William, I would say to myself," if William died, I could die too." But I knew that if I ended my own life I wouldn't be with him or with Jesus.

Every morning , the second my eyes opened, my mind would fly to the cemetery . It was torture. I would tell God that if I had to go one more day like this, I wouldn't be able to survive . I would walk the levee and I would weep, and moan and cry and groan.

Someone had told me that William had been seeing a girl that lived some streets over, and a while back that the girl had had a child. I went trying to look her up. Oh, if only this was true. I would have a part of him to hold on to. That turned out to be a false lead.

The detectives were still investigating the case. I couldn't bear to hear anything they had to report. Any news would be like twisting a knife in that raw wound in my heart. They told me it was a grudge killing. The woman who had taken over the laundromat had a grudge against William. Her son that worked offshore had accosted him with a board, I'm told, and William took it away from him twice, to avoid a fight. The third time, William defended himself by using the board on the other guy. The young man ran to his mother and then she gave him a gun to go after William. He hopped the ship after shooting William.

I never carried the burden of hating, resenting ,or even thinking about the guy that killed my son. I just wanted my child back.

155

Nothing, nothing could comfort me. I received cards with money from friends and Church members, who cared deeply and wanted to bring me some me kind of solace .But that meant absolutely nothing to me at that time. I just wanted my child back.

It was so lonely. I would think at times, if I only had a husband, someone to hold me, it would help me through this. But even in my state of misery and loneliness I knew it had to be a husband not just any man.

So many times, in the time of grief people will turn to many things trying to fill that empty place. Some turn to alcohol, drugs, illicit sex, etcetera. Some just grieve to death. The Holy Ghost was still working in my life and he was keeping me.

Horrible things were going on with me.

William had worn a cap that was still in the house I would smell his scent in that cap, and it brought me a little comfort, for the moment. I had heard this from others who lost loved ones, so I felt less weird. There was a huge picture of William's graduation hanging on the wall. I had to eventually take it down. This upset Kendrick, but it was too painful for me to look at it

When William was killed, he was wearing a brown and yellow striped polo shirt. Unless you have experienced this you cannot relate. Any time I laid my eyes on someone wearing a stripped tee shirt, I would feel the bullet in my chest. Another thing, I would go into a frenzy if I saw a gun on tv or anywhere else. I thought I was losing it until I found a support group "Parents Of Murdered Children." (POMC).

Support Group

No one else that was in my circle, could relate to what I was going through. No one I knew had lost a child. Everyone was running from me. I began to blame others for Williams death. I even blamed God, and thought I was a horrible person for doing so. There were times when others would get up and testify how their child had gotten shot, or was in some kind of accident, and was at the point of death, but lived.

I voiced my disappointment out loud. It was not fair, God had respect of person. Why didn't my Son live? I would think this every time I heard of a situation like this. I couldn't pray anymore. When I mentioned my concerns about my other son, Kendrick was on a downward path it was suggested that " You just have to pray for him."

My answer was "Why pray, I prayed for William." I don't know if I was bitter, but I was definitely resentful. I blamed William for letting them kill him. I asked him "Why did you let them kill you?"

I surely acted like someone who was a little touched in the head, until I attended the support group. Blame, anger, denial are all stages of grief. In the support group, every one of us had experienced most of the same feelings. I learned that I was not crazy. I learned that it was okay to be angry at God, for a while. He is a man of sorrow, and He is aquatinted with grief

I received help from the support group that helped me over a hump. Within the group each one was assigned a mentor. I was assigned to a big burly guy named R.J. He was a photographer and media reporter for the police department.

He had lost his son to violence. Someone had snatched his son's girlfriend's purse while they were walking through the French Quarters. His son pursued him, and a guy turned around and shot him in the chest.

Most of the members of the group had been attending a long time. I was new, and I was starving for all the information I could gobble up that would help me through this hell I was going through.

One night when I went they were discussing politics, or something. My insides were screaming for them to get on with the discussion on dealing with my problems. I understood, again why William had run away from church that night. I jumped up and ran out of the room. It was vital that I get what I had come for.

I soon stopped the group , but I kept in touch with R.J.

The main reason I couldn't continue was even though it was help to me, it was not a Christian group and it seemed like everyone in the room was smoking cigarettes. The room would fill with smoke and ever since I had received the Holy Ghost I had not had another cigarette. The smoke made me deathly ill. Who was I to tell them not to smoke. So, I gathered all the self-help literature I could find and did the best I could.

Huge Dark Hole

It was as if I was in this huge dark hole. I was in the world all alone. I felt that everyone should be able to see and feel my grief. Once, I was inconspicuously driving up a one-way street. The policeman yelled profanities at me for doing so. I thought to myself, "Doesn't he understand? I just lost my child!

I sought for someone, anyone who would listen to me at night, until my tongue got so heavy I could no longer speak.

For, hours. I would talk about William, and memories, and I couldn't stop crying. There was this raw, infectious hole in my heart where William had been, and it would not heal.

Quite often, in the time of grief, all a person needs is for someone to listen. People can say the wrong things in trying to comfort the griever. If they have not suffered what you have gone through it and it can leave you in a worse state than you were in, before they opened their mouths.

Once my listening ear, Raymond, said to me, "Sister Vergie, William is gone. You need to let him go." He meant well, but that did not sit well with me. It just twisted the knife that was in my heart. How did he

159

know? He never lost a child. He never even had a child. I was finished talking to him.

But, of course that didn't last I did continue, but I held back some of my feeling after that. It seemed everyone else would run from me. I would keep a bag packed, hoping someone would invite me to spend the night. One evening, I walked into my sister's home with my bag. She looked at me and asked, "Where are you going?" I walked right back out of the door. I was crushed. How could she be so cruel? Grieving the loss of a loved one is so surreal.

I remember for a long time, I learned, through reading and talking to others who had lost loved ones, that people will run from you and avoid you because they can't handle your tragedy. My sister cared deeply for me, but could not handle my hurt and pain. This is why a support group is so beneficial.

I tried to reach out to my oldest son, but every time I mentioned the subject, he would run. None of my family would have anything to do with me. I wondered, "Why is my life going this way, when all I ever wanted to do was live for God?" Ever since I found out that I was lost and on my way to Hell, all I wanted to do was live for God and do His will.

Why was this happening to me? I was devastated. How could I know that God was working out His plan in me? I was indeed being put through the fiery furnace. I finally went to my son and said, "Lawrence, I need your help. I can't go through this alone."

He told me, "Ma! I can't talk about it. It is too depressing." Then I realized that this was his way of grieving. This was also the worst way to grieve. It is best to find someone who will listen when you need to talk. There will be times when you can't bear for anyone to bring it up, but other times you have this desperate need to talk and pour out your, heart.

No one came to visit me. Not even the children wanted to be near me. One weekend, I tried to solicit the company of my little niece, Shelita, and my grandson, Cory. They were both dropped off at my home. Shelita cried for her Mom, my sister Betty, to come and pick her up and when she came for her, Cory cried to go with them.

There I was all alone. I felt so lost. I was so alone, and so lonely. I have never known loneliness like I felt in those years of grief. Having the desire to be held, as I mentioned earlier, " If I had have someone of my own who would hold me, I wouldn't be so lonely..

While in my healing process God dictated to me a series of songs. I could never deny that they came from a supernatural source. One of the songs is " Joy Cometh in The Morning." One line says, "He'll pick you up and He'll hold you, He'll rock you in His arms." He was the one that I needed to hold me, and He did.

But I was angry with Him. I felt God had cheated me out of my son. In the support group I learned if you are angry with God, don't be afraid to express your feelings.

It says in **Isaiah 53:3-4** He is despised and rejected of men; a man of sorrows and acquainted with grief. Surely he hath borne our griefs, and carried our sorrows.

Sometime later, this Scripture came to me that I read in a hotel room in Springfield, Connecticut, while on a manager's training trip for Stanley Home Products, **Isaiah 54:5-8** For thy Maker is thine husband; the Lord of hosts is his name; and thy Redeemer the Holy One of Israel; The God of the whole earth shall he be called. For the Lord hath called thee as a woman forsaken and grieved in spirit, and a wife of youth, when thou wast refused, saith thy God. For a small moment have I forsaken thee; but with great mercies will I gather thee.

In a little wrath I hid my face from thee for a moment; but with everlasting kindness will I have mercy on thee, saith the Lord thy Redeemer.

Also read **verse 13** … And all thy children shall be taught of the Lord; and great shall be the peace of thy children.

Finally, William was at peace.

A State of Depression

One thing that brought me comfort for a brief period of time was singing .However, being a part of the choir had its ups and downs. When certain songs were sun it took all, I had to remain on the choir stand.

There was a song that my son Lawrence lead with a female named Sylvia. Whenever we sang it seems like it would hit a raw spot in my heart. The lyrics were meant to minister to me, but it was before its time. This song is by the La. Mass choir:

My life was torn beyond repair

I felt so alone, seemed no one cared

You came along, gave me a song

To ease the pain and erase the strain

You could have left me standing there

With no one, no one to care

But You promised me You'd be there on time

And You did just what You said

Against all odds, I made the choice

To give You my life, now I rejoice

You answered my prayers not a moment too soon

Your word I embraced, my sins You erased

You could have left me standing there

With no one, no one to care

But You promised me You'd be there on time

And You did just what You said

163

Vergie Iglus

That's when You bless me
(Oh, I let it go) That's when You bless me
(Lord, You brought me through, now I'm brand new)
Yes, That's when You bless me.
(Oh, I'm here to stay) That's when You bless me...

If you are facing a trial of some sort, you will really appreciate the lyrics when you hear set to music

On occasions when we were on programs to sing, we would be lined up to go on stage, I would suddenly break down it was if this one person, a young lady, who seemed to always be watching over me. It was the choir director's wife, Lena, she was so kind, sweet, caring, and compassionate. She would leave her place in line and come and put her arms around me and comfort me. I will be forever grateful for her love and kindness to me in those trying times. A few years later, her family suffered the same kind of loss as I had. Her mother lost a young son.

While traveling I would break down on the bus. One night as we were traveling, another choir member named Janae, seeing my struggle, came to me saying," Sister Vergie, my mother has gone through what you're going through," and began to minister to me.

Janae's only brother had been killed by the police. How grateful I was, not for their loss, but for someone to share my feeling with., someone who understood. I couldn't wait to connect with her mother. I contacted her and we became friends. And even though we are hundreds of miles apart, she is in California and me in Louisiana, we are still best friends.

I was in a total state of depression. From time to time, I would meet people that I hadn't seen in a while and hadn't heard of Williams death. They would ask "How are the boys.?"

There were times I would say, " Oh, they're fine" That was not a lie. The two that I had left were fine. I dared not bring up the subject of William being gone; I would fall apart. Other times I would answer, "You know I lost one of my sons."

There are times when you just have to talk about it, and there are times when you can't bear to talk about it. That is why it's so important not to initiate the conversation when dealing with the grieving person.

There was the time when the investigation was going on I wanted to know if William had any last words. It took me a long time to ask, because I really didn't want to know.

The detective hesitated to tell me, and I was sorry I asked. He had pleaded for his life. That is a memory that will never go away. On upcoming holidays, I had to leave town. It was too painful for me to be the same city where he was killed. I had the desire to leave New Orleans for good. I don't know what kept me there.

There are times when you just have to be in a crowd, and sometimes you have to be alone. It can be so lonely even though you're in the midst of a crowd. I remember times when there were events given by the church or some group that I was invited to, where everyone was having fun, and all of a sudden I had to take off running. I had to be alone somewhere so I could break down, and let it all out.

I would try to reason with myself. I told myself that I was not the only one who had lost a loved one. I needed to have compassion for those grieving parents who had lost their children to the war in Vietnam

I would think of the former pastors wife who was grieving deeply for her husband. There would be times when she would light out of the church crying. That was not for the lost a child, but it was her loss just the same.

I knew I couldn't go on much longer in this state of mind. Pastor Cupit would minister to me as much as he knew how. He set up special appointments for me to try and bring some sort of solace to my mind. There was one thing he said to me that eased the pain a little. I was always looking for some words , some confirmation that what happened to William was the will of God.

During one of our conferences he said to me " Sister Vergie, how do we know if God didn't know William would be better off if he took him home."

I held on to that thought. It must have been his will. Healing doesn't happen overnight. Like grieving, it is a process.

I was still promoting swimming pools in the malls. One day I was worked in the Lake Forest Mall, and a young man passed by, he looked just like William. I left my post, ran to get in front of him so I could see his face.

Yes! To see if it was William. I knew if I shared this with anyone who couldn't relate they would surely think I must be going off the deep end. So, I called my mentor, R.J. I was desperate. He was not shocked ,or surprised in turn he said, "Vergie, that's incredible. Let me read you something. " He went on to read to me what he had written. We were encouraged to write down our experiences and feelings.

He goes on to tell me how he would be walking his dog in the park and he would spot a young man that resembled his son. He would run to catch up with him to see if was really his son. This happened on several occasions.

So, you see, it is very beneficial to attend a support group. You will hear some real crazy things that will make you realize that you are not really crazy. But they are coming from others who have suffered what you have suffered, and only they can relate to what you are feeling.

A Shimmer of Light

I was still battling grief and depression. I had no joy, no peace, no happiness. I spent holidays alone and cried, drowning in my loneliness and despair I had no relationship with my family. My sister Betty and her family had long since moved to Florida. I was so lost and so desperate.

I still felt robbed of the opportunity to touch my son for the last time. It left a void in my heart that needed to be filled. So, I longed to have a dream, just so I could hug him one last time. I asked God to give me a dream, but when I dreamt of him I could never get close to him. He was always far off.

One night I saw him at my Aunt Rosie Lee's house. She was my Dad's sister who had taken my sister Betty when Mom passed away. He was lying in the grass in her yard. He was wearing the royal blue suit with the black velvet collar that he looked so handsome in.

He raised up his head, and said to me in his deep, husky voice , "Mama, I wanted to preach." I had mixed emotions about this dream. I was so disappointed that he didn't get his opportunity to do what God had for him to do. Yet I was pleased to hear that it was his desire to fulfil his calling. The dream was very comforting in that way.

Finally, I had a dream where I was able to hug him. It was a vivid dream. It felt as if I had really touched him in the flesh. Thank you Jesus, for granting my heart's desire. This brought some sort of closure to me. God was so good to let me have this dream.

I will never forget the Sunday I was on one side of the choir stand singing either for Worship Service, or the Altar call. I looked up to see the guest bass guitarist; he looked just like William, dark complexion, and curly hair at the base of the neck. My heart skipped a few beats. I got rid of the mike somehow and I headed for the door.

One of the Sisters, Gwen Mack, noticed me leaving and caught up with me. She asked where I was going. I was hysterical ,but managed to get out the words. "That boy, he looks just like William."

She urged me not to leave. " Go in Pastor Cupit office and talk with him" I did. Pastor Cupit would have traded his heart for mine a long time ago if he could have. He was one of the most kind, honest, caring, humble, and compassionate Men of God, I have ever known.

Most people don't realize that pastors and their families all go through hardships, and sometimes persecutions, especially if they are taking a stance and upholding the word of God as is required.

I happen to know of some struggles Pastor Cupit was facing, and I wrote him a letter of encouragement. One day he called me and said, "Sister Vergie, I'm sitting here reading your letter for the third time. You have the gift of encouragement."

After God had given me the songs for my first CD, I went to the First Pentecostal to sing. Upon finishing he asked me, "Where did you get those words. "I told him it was the Holy Ghost. Somehow I felt that God's approval was upon what He had given me. It seemed like Pastor Cupit was saying, "This has got to be Holy Ghost ordained.

One day, after the episode at church concerning the bass player who looked like William , I knew if I was to survive, I had to turn back to the only one who could help me. The few people that had tried to comfort me, as sincere as they were, had failed to bring comfort. The rest had run from me. I knew I couldn't go on much longer in this state of mind.

There were times when I imagined that I was having a bad dream. And that I would wake up and William would be there. But painfully, regretfully, it was all too real. I determined in my heart that somehow, some way, I had to put a stop to this thing that was eating me alive. There had to be a way. This is when the end of the grieving process began to come to an end.

Heading For a Healing

God had given me the desire of my heart He had let me touch my son, even if was only a dream. My friend Ethel tried to comfort me and failed in her effort. She had since lost her husband Kenneth. She told me that I needed to do what she had done to help deal with her grief. She said I needed to go to the graveyard and say goodbye to William. I was ready to do whatever it took. So, she took me there. I truly cannot say if that helped at all.

It was then that I began to realize that if I was going to get through this constant agony that was tormenting me, there was only one source that I could turn to. And that was God and Him alone. So, I began to talk to him.

Hear me when I call, O God of my righteousness: Thou hast enlarged me when I was in distress; have mercy upon me, and hear my prayer. I prayed...How long wilt thou forget me O Lord forever? How long wilt thou hide thy face from me? How long shall I take counsel in my soul, having sorrow in my heart daily? How long shall mine enemy be exalted over me? **Psalm 4:1-2**

Consider and hear me, O Lord my God: lighten mine eyes, lest I sleep the sleep of death; Lest mine enemy say, I have prevailed against him; and those that trouble me rejoice when I am moved. But I have trusted in thy mercy; my heart shall rejoice in thy salvation. I will sing unto the Lord, because he hath dealt bountifully with me. **Psalm 13:1-6**

Now I was desperate to get relief from all this misery. I started reading my Bible diligently. God lead me to the following scriptures in **Philippians 4:4-8** ... Rejoice in the Lord always. I will say it again: Rejoice! Let your gentleness be evident to all. The Lord is near do not be anxious about anything, but in every situation, by prayer and petition, with thanksgiving, present your requests to God. And the peace of God ,which transcends all understanding, will guard your hearts and your minds in Christ Jesus. Finally, brothers and sisters, whatever is true, whatever is noble, whatever is right, whatever is pure, whatever is lovely, whatever is admirable—if anything is excellent or praiseworthy—think about such things. **Philippians 4: 4- 8.**

I read and reread that scripture every single day, more than once. Every time my mind would wander off on sad thoughts about William, I would create an imaginary hand in my mind. I would take that hand and twist my mind back to think on good things.

Gradually, slowly, I began to experience a lightening of the heaviness. The depression was lifting a little. I would think of something funny about William, and I would smile. I didn't go into hysterics before a holiday, or before his birthday.

It was God, ordering my steps.

Healing from grief is a process. It does not happen overnight. But it does begin. I remember the exact day, the place, and the time when my healing began. I was delivering a Stanley order to a customer uptown, about 5:30 on a Tuesday afternoon. As I got on the overpass on Broad Street, I was getting this done before church time, that night I felt this breakthrough. I was ready to give it all up.

This song by the Lanny Wolf Trio started singing in my spirit, and soon I was vocalizing it.

Lord you know I need a brand new touch,

My strength from yesterday is gone,

If you give me Lord another touch,

I'll have the strength to carry on.

Something happened that evening that was beyond me. Something drove me to the church, once inside I ran to the altar, something I was not able to do before. I fell on my knees and began to cry to God to restore me. Pastor Cupit and Brother Raymond both rushed to my side to pray with me.

I was on my way to a healing! Hallelujah!!

The Effects of Rejection and Abandonment

I gave up the house on Reynes street it held too many memories. I had given up on a lot . I had just got to the level to qualify for a retirement plan with Stanley Home Products, but I just couldn't focus on building a business anymore. I moved into an apartment in New Orleans East.

Terry was still a huge part of my life. Even though I had begun to heal from my grief over my son, I still had this terrible burden for this precious little boy. I carried him in my heart, and I held him in my arms. I prayed for him, and cried with him.

I would have given him a new Daddy if that had been possible. I didn't understand then why God would place such a burden on me after all I had to endure. My heart would break for him as he cried out for his dad. Terry was the first of many children God would place in my care. I had me on the wheel, or maybe He was molding and shaping me, getting me ready for the fire, it was...

"God's Perfect Plan." The older he became, the more he longed for his Dad. In addition to suffering from the rejection, Terry was hurting

173

deeply from the lack of attention from his mother. She brought men into her home and Terry witnessed what went on between them. He would call me and tell me every graphic detail of what he witnessed.. It was too much for a child's little mind to handle. It would break my heart. I would go get him, and remove him from the situation.

He called me one day and said, "Grand Ma, you know why I'm saving my money? I'm saving enough so me and my Mommy can move out of the projects." He had been saving some quarters from his allowance.

Once again, my heart was torn to pieces. I told him that he and I would pray that God would move them out of that place. He would run around the apartment checking the windows and doors, making sure they were locked. He would check the stove, making sure it was off. He was only six years old with all this responsibility.

Then there was the time he called me his voice filled with fear. He said there was a guy running loose in the projects with a gun, and the police were after him. He wanted me to come get him. I was at his every beck and call. He had, this empty place in his heart that only his dad could fill.

Then there was the time he called me, and the sound I heard was unreal . He was on the floor making a sound like a wounded animal. I heard him whimpering, making a low feeble sound expressing fear, pain and unhappiness He wanted me to come and get him The man that was with his mother at that time had held him down with his foot while his mother beat him with a belt.

Why didn't I report this abuse? All I could think of was just to love him, protect him, and keep him as close to me as I possibly could. That incident was so traumatic, he blocked it out. Once I mentioned it to him, and he didn't remember it.

Sometime later he was trying to play on the football team at his school, he kept having trouble with his leg. I took him to get it checked out. And an ex-ray revealed that he had a hairline fracture. The Doctor asked me if he had injured it somehow. I couldn't think of anything. When we were leaving he said to me ,"Grand Maw, that was the time Robert held me down with his foot, and my Mommy beat me with a belt."

My heart was so tender , I would feel every pain, all the hurt and anguish that he felt. All I could do was love him, pray for him and hold him. He was reacting to other men taking the place of his daddy, and his mother was adding to the pain abusing him along with the men.

He is suffering the effects of that tragic childhood today. But all I have ever heard from the responsible parties is that " he needs to grow up." No ! He needs to know that the most important person to him loves him. He needs to heal from all of those wounds that was inflicted upon him as a child.

How can any child ever survive that kind of treatment?

Rejection, abandonment ,and abuse that is a monster. A child should be able to know and feel the love of everyone around them, especially their parents.

Children are most precious in the sight of Jesus. Children are a gift from God. It is important to him how we raise and nurture them. Jesus said unless you become as a little child you cannot enter into the Kingdom.

WORKING THROUGH GRIEF

I was still in the process of my healing when friends, church members and acquaintances began to experience the loss of their children through acts of violence. As I began to minister to each of them, I realized that God had orchestrated the tests and the trials that He had allowed me to face.

Pastor Cupit encouraged me to form a Support Group which I named "Working Through Grief " My heart was broken for those who had lost their loved ones. I could empathize with them. I could truthfully say "I know what you are feeling." And they could empathize with me.

Grief is a process and it takes time. There is nothing immoral about your grief. Your feelings are your own, and they are real. No one can tell you how to grieve, or how long to grieve. There are no quick fixes to grief.

You don't have to make apologize for your feelings. That is why it is so important to locate someone who is willing to just listen. If you suppress your feelings they will surface one way or the other.

My grief never surfaced in the form of anger or bitterness against anyone that I came in contact with or even against the person who killed my son.

You are not lacking in your faith because you are feeling sorrow. The use of alcohol or drugs is detrimental to your recovery from grief. During my most severe stages of grief, when it seemed I would lose my mind, a doctor offered me some sleeping pills to help me sleep and I refused. I thank my God that I did. Who knows what that would have led to? God had designed this, and He knew that in the process of time I would turn to the only source that could give me lasting peace, Himself.

You don't have to make other people comfortable by denying yourself the right to grieve. After going through, and coming out of what I went through proves that I am a survivor . If you are going through a process know that you are a survivor, or you wouldn't be here.

There is no end to God's power, and you can draw from that power. No matter how painful how intense or profound the suffering is; I am a witness, it does get better. The light will eventually begin to shine through.

Remember this too will pass.

There are those times when some people in your circle of acquaintance have experienced that kind of loss, and you find yourself in a position to provide comfort for them. This is where you take off running. Or in your effort to help you end up saying the wrong thing. Neither one of these actions is helpful to the hurting.

This is why it's so important in our dealings with people no matter what their situation is whether we are dealing with children or adults. Whether we are ministering, or witnessing.

Words have power! It matters not what comes out of our mouth. So many times, I have opened my mouth, in other types of situations, and after the words came out, I felt like I had put my foot in it. whether they are well meaning or not, words once spoken cannot be recalled. They can bring harm to the ones to whom they are spoken.

We must be sensitive to the feelings of others. Words have the power to build up, or tear down. Ministering to the grieving calls for commitment.. There are times when they cannot sleep. If you sincerely want to help, you must sacrifice your sleep, and your time.

I remember when my friend would call me in the middle of the night to vent. She was not hurting from the loss of a loved one, but she was hurting just the same and I would listen.

You must be there to help them through these difficult times. The pain won't wait till the morning comes. People have a tendency to leave the grieving people all alone. Don't desert them after the funeral.

Everyone went home and left me alone and forsaken. I had never felt so desolate, and alone. I learned later that they can't handle your pain. You don't need to try and fix the pain. There has to be pain before a healing.

If the bereaved doesn't grieve properly, they cannot heal. You have heard the saying," No pain, no gain, " well in the case of grieving it is certainly a true statement.

Never initiate the conversation when attempting to comfort someone who is grieving the loss of a loved one. There are times when the person will be desperate to talk, and talk, and rattle off, even things that won't make sense. They just need your ear. It is not necessary to speak a word. Once a well-meaning person said something to me, thinking it would bring comfort, but instead it had the opposite effect. She had not said what I wanted to hear. You can't possibly know what's going on inside of their torn and shattered heart. Just be there and listen with a nod, make a sound of some kind. Looking them in the eye, acknowledging that you are interested.

Many times, people will say "I know how you feel" without having had the same or similar experience. They can't possibly know, they might say, "I can imagine how hard this must be," but they don't know, however well-meaning their words of comfort might be.

Vergie Iglus

There are times when the griever will not want to hear, or speak a word about their loved ones, sometimes it is too painful to talk about their loss. Let them bring it up, and you listen.

There were times when someone who hadn't heard about William would ask about my boys, I would say , they are fine, and quickly change the subject . At other time I would say, "You know I lost one of my sons" and would be ready for an ear. There were times I had to be in a crowd, and other times I ran from the the crowd to be alone to grieve. Don't do all the talking.

Oh, how I needed to get my feelings out that night at the support group. They were talking politics, and my grief was consuming me. When I couldn't take anymore, I jumped up and ran out of the room.

Be sincere, don't pretend to be sincere. A person can tell if you are really listening, so you must listen with the heart. Grieving is a matter of the heart and not the head. Many times, I would be in desperate need to get my feelings out and the person would show a disinterest or change the conversation. This can be devastating to the griever.

Again, you don't need to say anything. Being there is more important than knowing what to say. Let all of the feelings come out. Nothing is shocking or silly, or awful thinking. Feelings are feelings. There are no right or wrong feelings.

Grief is acute sorrow, deep suffering, and profound sadness. It is our attempt to recover from our loss, and recovery will come. God has not forsaken us. He is working out His perfect plan in us.

F E A R... False Evidence Appearing Real

After my healing began, grief was still playing a big part in my life. Even in Macon things had not gone well at all with Kendrick. He just couldn't seem to overcome his grief and I was worried about him. And yes, I even feared for his life.

He was acting unstable and Destiny was worried also. She reached out to me and did what she thought would help. She sent her daughter, Trudy to get his little son Terry to visit him, hoping that would bring some comfort. That too, was a failed effort.

She then invited me to come for a visit. hoping that Kendrick and I might be able to comfort each other. That did not help. a short time later, he was hopping freight trains going from place to place. She called me and told me he was sleeping in the graveyard.

One day she called me and told me he had left home and was passing through New Orleans to see his son, before going on to California to be with Terry's uncle who was a Preacher. This brought me a ray of hope. At least he was reaching out to someone who'd be a positive resource. I waited and waited for him to call or show up, but he never did.

I was worried. What had happened to him? I was so anxious to see him, but he never showed up. I was so worried, I was frantic. At the same time, I was waiting for him to show up I had heard on the news about a killing in the Desire Housing project. The description fit my Kendrick to a tee.

The report described height, a mark on his thigh , and he was dressed in layers. My heart fell in my stomach. Oh! what grief won't take you through . I called Destiny and asked her did Kendrick have a mark on his thigh. She said, "a big one."

I told her about the news and described how he was dressed, and she said that's the way he dressed.

I told her that someone had killed him. She was shocked, and asked " Why did he let them kill him? what a question. the same one I asked when it happened to William. And I blamed William for letting it happen to him.

What did I do next? I called Pastor Watson to arrange a private funeral and asked him not to announce it. I was thinking how everyone would think what a horrible mother I was to have two sons be murdered. I called Pastor Watson's mother and told her what had happened.

Destiny and I were on the phone one day making plans for a dismissal for Kendrick. One day while we were on the phone we were interrupted by an incoming call. Before I could answer it hung up. we both said " that sounded like Kendrick."

I can't remember if it was the same day or the next, that he called. what bliss. there was joy unspeakable. and full of glory. He was headed to California, indeed. He was very much alive.

Destiny and I convinced him to turn around and come to New Orleans and she would leave Macon and meet him there. It didn't take much convincing. I sent him a plane ticket and he came to live with me.

I just knew if I got him there and got him to Church, things would be different. That was the one stipulation to his living with me again, that he had to go to church on Sunday's and he went This also gave Terry an opportunity to spend some quality time with his dad. He would lift his hands straight up and praise God as if trying to touch him physically, it seemed.

He reminded me of myself. When we hit rock bottom, there is no way out but up. He was reaching out to God for help. I could see the desperation he displayed. He was faithful in going to church. He would get ready before I was ready, anxious to leave. There was a sister in church who had tried to befriend him. not knowing he was married. He was trying to get as close to God as he could and better himself to be reunited with his wife.

So, the time came when Destiny had finalized things in Macon, and she and Trudy were ready to come back to New Orleans. .I paid a deposit on an apartment, and rented a U-Haul that Kendrick drove to Macon to move them.

Before they could move into the apartment, they had to pay the first month's rent. Destiny came to me complaining how the Landlord was demanding it, and could I pay it.

Everyone knew me as a person who could never say no. But this time I felt, "This is too much," And I said "No!!" She immediately began to shun me.

A Child Scorned

Destiny was still shunning me because I would not pay her rent at the apartment. There was something way off with her. She had a child but forbad Kendrick to be near him. In his weak, and vulnerable state he compiled. He had to be compliant to her every command. So, he couldn't have any relationship with his little boy. And of course, he had to shun me as well

She would threaten to divorce him or leave and go back to her country. She came to me one day to tell me among other things that Kendrick was getting closer to God than she was. She explained that , "He raising he hands and all."

And she told me of something else he did that displeased her and " I cussed he out, right in church ," like I said, something was way off with her.

She soon pulled him out of church, and I didn't see much of them anymore. That was also another way to keep him from seeing his child. In spite of it all Terry was suffering.

There was a tragic event that took place in his little life when he was eight years old. I was always trying to fix his life any way I could.

I had registered him for Kids Camp in Tioga, Louisiana, he would be going with a group of other kids. Hopefully he would have a good time there and it would take his mind off what was bringing him so much pain. And prayerfully God would touch him and deliver him from it all.

Just before it was time for him to be picked up, his Mom called and asked to speak to him. A few seconds later I saw him grab his stomach in pain. Without an ounce of wisdom, she had announced to him on the phone that his favorite little cousin, Kennedy had just gotten run over by a car and was killed. He went into shock. Lord! How much more?

Little Kennedy was eight years old, the same age as himself. He pulled himself together enough to go to Camp. He came back sharing his adventures of shaving cream fights.

But he was seldom happy, I know this sounds unbelievable ,but it is the absolute truth. It is because the horrible reality of the suffering, and heartache that little children endure at the hands of parents who bring them into this world, and then just throw them away. Other than that, these events would not be in my book.

Whatever was inflicted upon me doesn't matter. But my heart still aches for the children whom God placed in my care.

My prayer is that someone who reads this book will realize the seriousness of the abandonment and rejection of a child. Maybe you may have a loving adoring, happy home where there is one parent, or two parents involved. Whatever the case may be the Child/Children feel loved, and protected. You cannot imagine a child being unloved, unwanted and unprotected from the insecurities and everything else that life throws their way.

Maybe you can find it in your hearts to reach out to some hurting, rejected, abandoned child that needs love. To witness the aftermath of the rejection, is a constant burden on my heart.

Now that I have explained why I am including this portion in this book; I will move on to the rest of the story. Destiny had no conscious at all. I had never met anyone quite like her. She had committed this ungodly act while in the choir having cussed out all the leadership starting with the Pastor. She had cussed me out for not taking her side. She had no feelings at all for an innocent child, and no use for anyone that did not serve her purpose..

I continued to pray for both she and Kendrick. We were two blocks from each other, but Terry was not allowed to see his dad. One evening while passing by their apartment I got bold enough to knock on the door. I was going to let him see his dad and I would suffer the consequences.

We got out of the car and knocked on the door the television was on, but no one answered the door . I told him that no one was home. He pointed out to me that the TV was on. Once again I tried to lighten his disappointment by telling him that people leave their TVs on to discourage anyone from breaking into their home when they are not at home. Which was the truth.

If only a mother or a father could feel the pain of rejection that a child feels when they make the decisions to abandon them. It is so devastating to a child that without God's intervention, they will never survive it.

My heart still breaks for a child, any child, that I know who is suffering from the lack of love and care from their mother and father. Many times, children who are rejected, as a child carry their problems into adulthood, marriages ,relationships, careers etc. and suffer because of this.

Terrence was a year old when William died. That little boy became a brand in my heart, he was my rock. We were inseparable. The bond between us was unexplainable. He would express his feelings to me concerning his dad. It was so heartbreaking. Sometimes I grieved for him no less than what I grieved for my own son William who had died.

The Separation and Reunion

One day Destiny call me to tell me that Kendrick was abusing drugs again, "bad." She had left him and told him that she was going back to her native country. My heart sank to my stomach. " How much more can I take Lord" I thought things were settling down. At least I thought he was physically sound. When would it all end? This time I knew what I had to do. Some of us would go to the church every morning for five o'clock prayer. Sis Watson, Sylvia, and I went together.

The next morning when I got to the church, I fell on my face before the Lord. "In my distress I called unto the Lord, and cried out to my God ; he heard my voice from His temple, And my cry came before Him, *even* to His ears. **Psalm 18:6 I** told God, " God, this is too hard for me. I can't handle this, but you can. I interceded for my Son. I stood in the gap for him.

When I finished praying that morning, and got up off my knees, there was not a worry in the world. I was light as a feather. I had taken my burdens to the feet of Jesus and I left them there. He had let me know that I could trust Him. I knew right then, and right there that Kendrick would be alright. This had a complete opposite effect on him. It was as he was shocked into reality. God had brought me through some hard times, and I had survived them. He was not about to leave me now.

I went through the "School of hard knocks "to learn what I have learned. Because of my past experiences I can encourage   others who are struggling with situations that have you burdened down to just let go, and let God. Really , really let go. He doesn't need our help.

I have always been a person who was a "fix it " person. I wanted to fix everything. It is because I never wanted to see anyone hurting. I still have those same traits, but it comes to the time when you realize that you must let go and let God have His way in a situation. He has no rival, he has no equal. He is God all by himself.

It is a process, and there may be many trials, but step by step , day by day you will get there. Just remember, if God can't do it, it can't be done.

Kendrick called me after I had prayed that morning to tell me that Destiny had moved out and was on her way to her home country. He said that she had taken his clothes. She would buy his clothes with his money, but I guess she considered them her clothes.

It was the most amazing thing. Kendrick had been known to fall apart at the least little change in his life. This time he was as calm as a cucumber, so to speak. He told me that Destiny had left him and expected him to fall apart but that he was not going to let this destroy him.

He was going to get his life together. He was not going to quit his job and was going to save his money. He was not going to keep the apartment. Once again he moved in with me. He gave me money every payday to deposit for him. My ultimate goal was to get him back in Church.

It turned out that Destiny and Trudy were living with a family from church. When she didn't get any news of his demise ,she came out of hiding and prompted Trudy to call his job to find out if he was still working What a surprise she was in for.

She found out that he was happily at work and not in an institution because of the breakup. He earned a very good salary on his job, and after all Trudy had to pay her tuition for college. He also helped her with her schoolwork . She instantly became friendly with me when she found out that he was living with me. She set up visitation.   Well, you know by now that I hold no grudges. I always believe that everything would improve and be better the next time around.

This time, it's going to be different. This time we will be a family this time, Terry will get to be with his Father. Destiny came over for the second visit and she never left. When Destiny moved in with me and Kenneth I was presently working at a home around the corner and down the streets from where we lived. It was run by Volunteers of America. It was only about four blocks in walking distance. But because I worked from six am to two pm, it was dark when I left home, so I drove to the Home. I recommended Destiny for a position there. She and I were hired for the same shift so, every morning I would give her a ride to work. An apartment became available right across the parking lot from me, and I spoke to my landlord in their behalf.

Destiny's Scheme

Terry continued to suffer for the lack of a relationship with his dad. He was still practically living with me. For a brief time, I had convinced Kendrick to spend a little time with Terry, and help a little with his homework. My primary purpose was to get him to spend some time with him. He came over for a couple of times and stayed for about twenty minutes and he was gone.

After she found out that he could be persuaded at least to acknowledge him, She took some drastic measures to prevent that from happening.

One of the things she did, I will not go into detail, without the proof of the matter. Even though I know it to be true. When that did not work out she adopted a baby girl. by some source, she set out to adopt a child. Seems one of the requirements was that she and Kendrick had to have physical contact and sign the documents. She couldn't get him to cooperate but in spite of his refusal, she brought a little baby girl home. In one month, no waiting period. She told me said she paid the price.

By now, she was working the two pm, to ten pm shift when Kendrick got home from work, he had to babysit. There would be no time for Terry.

She had no problem cussing me out, if I even looked the wrong way at her. I kept my mouth shut. It was a horrible situation.

Working in the Group Home

It was not long before Kenneth bought them a little car. So, she stopped riding with me and started driving her car. One day I suggested that since she was driving, I maybe could ride with her . We lived practically next door, and we were going the same place. She proudly announced to me in her native accent, "Kenneth don't want nobody riding in that car." They had moved in when the apartment was ready and that was the end of the "Fake Friendship."

She didn't need me for anything anymore. I was not allowed to go to her apartment , Terry was not allowed over there, and Kenneth was not allowed at my apartment.

At the Group Home, all hell broke loose. All of a sudden everyone started turning on me. The home consisted of six clients with mental disabilities. When I started I found the staff being abusive toward the clients.

They were hitting them with brooms and shoes. They also verbally abused them, but I spoke out against it. I reported it to the Home Manager. They were less open with their actions while I was there from then on.

But! Destiny entered the scene and they found out that she was connected to my family, and didn't like a bone in my body. It was a different story, every one of the staff started following her lead. There was one who secretly didn't agree with her but had to do it behind her back .

The staff all tried everything they could to provoke me daily. They were like imps vexing me when I was in their presence, they would start up a conversation that would make the devil hide his face.

When I remained quiet, I was asked by one of them," Vergie, why you ain't saying nothing?"

The Group Home consisted of six clients. There was always two clients assigned to one staff member. Each Staff was responsible for getting their client to their outings or appointments So there was always three staff remaining in the home for every shift.

Sometimes, we all had to ride in the van at the same time when taking the clients on outings. They would start up there very vulgar conversation to try and provoke me. They found out that cigarette smoke affected me, so they would light up in the closed van. When I would lower the window or fan the smoke, one would reply, "Whatcha fanning for ain't nobody that Holy ?"

I ignored every single thing they did to me, in their presence! But I was hurt, I was wounded, and I felt the evil words they tossed at me every day. But I was not about to let them get the pleasure of knowing I was hurting from their evil.

I could not wait till the end of the shift, and go home and talk, and cry to God. I would tell Him how I felt and what I was going through, as if He didn't see, as if He didn't know.

I prayed **Psalm 143:1**"Hear my prayer o Lord, Give ear to my supplications! In Your faithfulness answer me, *And* in Your righteousness."

The Lord heard my prayers, and He answered me through His word … Do not fret because of evildoers, Nor be envious of the workers of iniquity. For they shall soon be cut down like the grass, and wither as the green herb .

Trust in the Lord, and do good, Dwell in the land, and feed on His faithfulness. Delight yourself also in the Lord, and He shall give you the desires of your heart. Commit your way to the Lord, Trust also in Him, And He shall bring it to pass. He shall bring forth your righteousness as the light, and your justice as the noonday. Rest in the Lord, and wait patiently for Him; Do not fret because of him who prospers in his way, Because of the man who brings wicked schemes to pass .Cease from anger, and forsake wrath; Do not fret—it only causes harm.

For evildoers shall be cut off; But those who wait on the Lord, They shall inherit the earth. For yet a little while and the wicked shall be no more; Indeed, you will look carefully for his place, But it shall be no more.

The wicked plots against the just, And gnashes at him with his teeth. The Lord laughs at him, For He sees that his day is coming. The wicked have drawn the sword and have bent their bow, To cast down the poor and needy, to slay those who are of upright conduct. Their sword shall enter their own heart, And their bows shall be broken.

A little that a righteous man has is better than the riches of many wicked For the arms of the wicked shall be broken, But the Lord upholds the righteous. The Lord knows the days of the upright, And their inheritance shall be forever

They shall not be ashamed in the evil time, And in the days of famine they shall be satisfied. But the wicked shall perish; And the enemies of the Lord, Like the splendor of the meadows, shall vanish into smoke they shall vanish away. **Psalm 37: 1-20**

I was like a sheep amount wolves, but would go home, have my time with God, and I would go back to work the next day ,singing, as it if I didn't have a care in the world.

A Song in my Heart

I returned to work each day, with a song in my heart, and on my lips, instead of down and depressed. One of the Staff , Henrietta, would always tell me, "Vergie, you need to shut up, "Don't nobody wanna hear all that noise, you can't sing."

Then Destiny would break out with a tune, and was complimented with, " Oh Destiny, you have a beautiful voice." I ignored all of it. One day the House Manager presented a proposal to me.

She needed to fill the position of an Assistant House Manager. She asked if I would be interested. She told me that I was the only one in the home with common sense, her words! I accepted the offer, and she passed the information on to her supervisor. The staff got wind of the news and started a campaign to put a stop to it. They wrote anonymous letters to the supervisor, telling her that Darla had me taking over the house. They falsely accused her of awful things that was going on in the house.

The supervisor called a meeting with Darla and I. She told us of the letters and the accusations, which she knew to be false. She told me that Darla was acting with her heart, and not her head. If she allowed me to be promoted, that the crew would crucify me. "I am not in the business of promoting someone and having to bring them back down," she said.

So, there I was, again. This was the second time jealousy had played a part in an effort to prevent me from reaching my destiny.

But God had a "perfect plan."

When I was up for a promotion with Stanley Home Products I was told by my manager that if he promoted me I would be crucified, so my own branch was created, with the people that I had, and we grew from there.

It turned out that in this case, God was also directing my path, even though it seemed to be the opposite Darla was clearly disappointed that I could not take the position as Assistant House Manager. She called me a few days later with another offer. She asked , "Vergie, since you can't be Assistant Manager, would you like to be the Floater?"

When she explained the duties of a Floater, "Oh yes! I would like to be the Floater"

The duties of a Floater was to carry a pager that the company provided by volunteers from the Veterans of America. I would be on call to fill a shift whenever any Staff had to take off for some reason.

As a Floater, I had to be guaranteed forty hours. So, Darla assigned me the duties of cooking every day for the home, which included clients, and staff. We ate our meals in the home. I worked very seldom at nights, and hardly any Sundays.

The plan of Satan had backfired. As a Floater, I could be paid overtime. I earned more as a floater, than I ever would have as Assistant Manager, I got my forty hours as cook, and worked some shifts which gave me the overtime.

God had done it again. As you continue to read, somewhere along the line you will be thinking by now that this must be a fiction book, but what you read really did happened in real life, my life.

It is not for sympathy or pity that I tell my story, but to show how one can survive whatever life throws our way, when God is doing life with us.

Surely He shall deliver you from the snare of the fowler And from the perilous pestilence. "He shall cover you with Him , And under His wings you shall take refuge; His truth shall be your shield and buckler "A thousand may fall at your side, And ten thousand at your right hand; But it shall not come near you." **Psalm 91: 3-4,7.**

They had set a snare for me, but I had made God my refuge and they couldn't harm me. But there was no giving up on their part. Read on…

The Power in Prayer

When the staff found out I had become the Floater, they were furious, especially Destiny. She was the ring- leader.
They devised a plan to get Darla fired, and they ate me alive, so to speak. There were anonymous letters that stated Darla was having orgies in the home, and any- thing else that they could conger up.

They did everything possible to provoke me. But I never revealed my hurt before them. I would go Home and pour out my heart to God, and He would lift the heavy burden that was in my heart

One morning Destiny was getting her Clients ready for School and was ironing their uniforms when she started rebuking me with a loud voice from the room she was in. Some of those words she used were "That's why your children don't want nothing to do with you now. You ain't had nothing but women all your life. You come in this room I'll knock you out with this iron. Then I'll see where yo Holy Ghost at."

She paused after each sentence waiting for me to respond. I said not a word. By this time, I was on the phone, either making or receiving a call. Then she threw her final blow. "You had a son get killed because of you," she screamed. She had hit a raw spot in my heart it felt like a knife was twisted inside of it. Yet, I never said a word. I went home at the end of the shift and talked to God, cried before Him.

The next day, I went to work with a song in my heart, and on my lips. The amazing thing about this, was that I didn't have to fake the peace that I felt. It was a real, true, genuine peace that God gave to me every time I went to Him.

Terry was still longing for his Dad. My heart still ached for him. I knew that Kendrick loved a certain kind of bread. So, I was in the bread store one day and saw the very kind he liked. It was a huge long loaf of thick sliced bread. I was always thinking of a way for Terry to get just a glimpse of his Dad, so I bought a loaf of bread.

I sent it to Kendrick by Terry. He took it at the door and sent him back across the parking without inviting him in. It was outrageous to have to take these kinds of measures for an innocent child to see his Father.

I do not not blame Destiny solely for this. It was the responsibility of the Father to stand up to his obligations and nurture his Son. To love him, and take care of him. There have been so many opportunities to step in and try to make some kind of amends, but no efforts have been made to this day.

People can be so selfish, and cold hearted. I will never understand how a Mother, or a Father could move on with their lives. Some seek other individuals who have Children. Again, it is not the fault of the other party. It is the responsibility of the parents. To see the hurt, the pain, the insecurities that is inflicted upon a child is unbearable for me to watch.

I know, because I lived through it with the child. With Face Book, and Social Media, everything can be seen by the child today even if they are in different states. Having been rejected, and abandoned, by a parent and to see the interactions with that parent with other children has a devastating effect. No matter how old they are, accept by the power of God, it is dealt with. Only He can heal that pain and hurt.

One day Darla came to me and told me, "Vergie. I didn't want to tell you this, but I thought you should know the reason why the Staff is not eating your cooking. Destiny told them not to eat your cooking because you practice Hoo-Doo. She said you sent her husband a loaf of bread and he threw it in the dumpster because it was Hoo-Dooed.

This news hit me like a bolt. It was not the lie about me that hit me so hard, it was the part that was the truth. I had sent my son a loaf of bread and he had thrown it in the dumpster. After I thought about it, It probably was all a lie. But I didn't dare approach my son with anything at all. He had to defend his wife in all things so I went home. I fell on my face before God. My heart was so broken. I told God; "God, I'm hurting and. I don't know what to do " I promise you, that just as I approached Him, he answered me back in the form of a song. It is an old song by Abertina Walker . " Hold your Peace"

Hold Your Peace, let the Lord fight your battle,

Hold your peace He will see you through.

The verse says. "Now if someone has done you wrong, just forgive them, and you go on, no matter whether great or small just forgive them and say Lord make me strong."

It goes to say what they don't know; they've got to reap just what they sow. What goes around sure will come around.. He will see you through. God spoke to me so plainly through that song. The words were so befitting. And it came with anointing and power.

We were having a prayer meeting that morning, which was a Saturday. I always lead the worship for us ladies wherever we gathered I was so hyped with the presence of God upon me, I called my Lady's Auxiliaries TPIP President, who was also my confidant and friend. She knew what I was going through. I told her of my experience. She said "

201

you will have to sing that song for Lady's Prayer. And I did. God moved in that place. Once again the Lord had performed a work in me.

The Exit

The Group Home was home for the Home Managers. They lived in half of the duplex. On Darla's off time she would do hair for her friends and family as well as her regular customers. The Staff watched her like a Hawk. You could walk into her residence anytime during the day if there was a question or a need for anything pertaining to the clients.

One day one of the staff walked in while she was doing a relatives hair. She had become hot and removed her shirt. I had gone over earlier and hardly noticed. When the Staff saw this it was ,"GOTTCHA."

She spread the word to the leader, Destiny and the others. They made their report to the Supervisor they added and subtracted, and made it appear nasty, and ugly.

Poor Darla! She had been a fair manager. She overlooked much of the drama that went on and tried to keep the peace. But they were like vultures. Out to prance upon their prey. This time they had succeeded. With so many complaints, actions had to be taken. So, Darla had to be let go.

The custom for firing someone from the home was as follows: The supervisor would call the police and have them escort you out the door and down the street. You were never permitted to darken that door again. It is degrading, and embarrassing. My heart went out to her. She really was a good person with a kind and compassionate heart, who cared about the clients.

A new manager, Patricia ,was brought in and she got an ear full. She received anonymous notes about me. That was their M.O. Before she could move in, she was looking at me as she had already judged and condemned me. She immediately took my pager! And preceded to put me on a schedule. I called a meeting with her in her office. I told her I knew that she had heard things about me, but please don't judge me by what no one else says. "Get to know me for yourself." I asked when she made the schedule if she scheduled me on Sunday , please schedule me from 6am to 2pm. My church started at 3pm.

I can't remember if she responded at all . But when the schedule went up she had me working every Sunday from 2pm, to 10pm. That meant I would miss every single Sunday service. Okay God, back to my praying ground. I talked to my friend, and I told him, God, if this is where you want me on Sunday's ,this is where I'll be. You must a purpose in it all.

Ok, brace yourself for this one. When I looked at the schedule the next day, I was not up to work not one single Sunday! Nobody can't tell me that prayer does not work. My God had done it again.

I was still being abused, and persecuted by the staff, but I was content. They continued to pile in the kitchen while I was cooking spewing out vulgarities and talking about events of all kinds of ungodly things, just to provoke me.. I knew God had my back.

One day Henrietta caught the bus to go home. She is the one who always told me I couldn't sing, and did her part in cussing me out. When she stepped down from the bus a car hit her and knocked her a few feet, she said. They talked about it, but no one made an effort to visit her. I noticed that her paycheck was laying there for a while.

I went and bought her a get well card took her check and brought it to her. Her attitude toward me changed from then on. However ,she had to keep a low profile in the presence of Destiny. But she never harassed me again, and I visited her several times while she was laid up.

The End of a Season

God had spoken to me, "Your season here is over." It was time for me to move on to my next test. I was informed of a training class right near me, for a Home Health Aide. Without saying a word to anyone, I took it. I was still being harassed by the staff. One of those girls was named Vanessa.

When I finished, I was assigned a patient with a company that was doing the training. I was working a two to ten shift at the home. I saw my patient at six in the morning. They paid $17.00 an hour, or per visit.

The first day I worked as a Home Health Aide; I was working on the two o'clock shift at the home. I showed up with my uniform on and my stethoscope around my neck.

Everyone's eyes got as big as quarters. I began to pick patients, and I was earning a very good salary at $17.00 per visit.

I kept working at the home until one day I was driving down Diamond Road to get to work at the home. I fell asleep at the wheel. God let me know, it's time. Your season has ended at the group home. Your mission is over.

God is so awesome; He is the great I am. If we put our trust in Him he will never let us down. Our God was not going to allow me to be escorted out of that home by any policeman. Plus, I could walk in that home any time I felt like it. And I did. Just to let them know what kind of God I Serve.

It was not long before one of the staff asked me what did I do to get this position. It was Vanessa. The one who cussed me out for no reason when she felt like it. I gave her the information and she went and took the training. But instead of doing Home Health, she became a lobotomist. I was really happy for her.

I have shared some of my experiences with some of my friends and others as a witness as to what God will do for those who will put their trust in him.

Some wonder and even ask, " How can you be so kind to someone who would treat you that way?" My reply, Jesus did it, and that is what He requires of me .Maybe some of the people who treated me badly are also wondering how can I treat them so kindly. They might be thinking I'm a fool for doing so. Receiving all of the, abuse, the reject, the criticism, the false accusations, and always coming back for more.

Well! "I am a fool. I say it with Paul, " I'm a fool for Christ" I am His servant, and I must obey Him."

Forgiving someone who has wronged you, loving someone who hates you, doing good for those despise you is an easy task if you . are truly a follower of Christ. That is what He did, and that is what He teaches us to do .

All of the efforts that the Staff had made to get me fired had failed. God was not going to let me be ashamed. I felt so safe in His arms. He had let me know That He would not leave me nor forsake me. He had been with me every step I f the way. Like Job said," Yet, He knows the way I have taken when He has tested, I shall come out as gold. **Job 23:10**.

Part 5

Vergie Iglus

My New Assignment

I did Home Health for about a year, but it was very hard work . I had accumulated a number of patients, and some of them were full care. There were others where you merely had to go in and take vital signs. At the end of the day I was burned out.

The Company where I took my training and my first assignment went under Home Health. At that time, it a very big business. Everyone and their uncle was opening a Home Health Company. But there was a lot of Medicaid fraud. So many of them were forced to close down.

I was struggling to keep up seeing so many patients in one day. I signed on with another company, but the pay wasn't as good. I heard of this foster care program with YWCA. I thought this was something I might want to try. I was still fighting the spirit of depression and loneliness. It was still just Terry and I ; we were a team. He still longed for his Dad and that grieved my heart. I was constantly trying to find ways to comfort him but nothing, or no one could fill that empty place in his heart.

So, I went to a meeting with YMCA, to see what this Foster Care was all about. I decided to try it, and right away I knew this was my next assignment. God had called me to foster trouble, abused, and hurting children.

This was also, another steppingstone for me .I could never have imagined what an impact this would have on my own life.

208

In my heart when I was informed about how something like this would help to fill the void that still remained in my heart God was dealing with me in steps. So, I signed up with YWCA, Young Women Christian Association) working within the department of TFC (Therapeutic Foster Care).

I joined a program that placed children into your home that had the worst problems. These children had been severely abused, physically and sexually. Some by their own parents. They were so damaged and broken that only God could deliver them. This had affected them mentally, and it was not at all an easy task to care for them. I was told often that it took a special kind of person to do what I was doing, and I could not disagree.

Everyone was not cut out for this, but like so many things that took place in my life, this was God ordained. In spite of the challenges of caring or these children, it was very therapeutic for me also.

The first child that was placed in my home was a little baby boy named Aaron. I thought "this was a piece of cake. He was nine months old, and I fell in love with him. However, his grandmother was taking classes to gain custody of him. I knew he would be leaving me soon. I only keep him nine months. It saddened my heart to see him go."

The second one didn't work out at all. So, I will tell about the third child that was placed in my home. It was a precious little girl that I will call Wanda, she was five years old. My home was qualified for two children, but little Wanda's' problems were so severe, she required individual attention.

In a few months, I was able to take other children. Even though my home was a two children home, the Y obtained a wavier so that I could take three children. I thought I specialized in teenage care, but I had taken from the age of nine months, to 17 years old .It was truly a challenge for any parent in TFC.

So, the ones that were in it for the money added to the destruction of the child. I witnessed several that were in it for the money. The TFC pay was more than double the amount of regular foster care. They would accept a child into their homes and the minute there was problem the child was out the door. They would just get another one. So, the child learned to reject the parent, before they became rejected.

They would come in so hungry for love ,but at the same time, afraid to trust you. But they would immediately began addressing you as Mama . I fostered for twelve years, and only God gave me the strength and endurance to do so.

I could never write everything in this book of what it's like too to be a parent to these troubled kids. I was cursed out, bitten, spit on. I've had my belongings broken up, thrown out the door.

At age fourteen Wanda's imbedded problems began to surface. One night I was trying to restrain her as she was in a position to hurt herself, or someone else. She was acting out and I experienced a real demon.

I demanded him to come out in the name of Jesus. He spoke back in a deep, deep voice, that you knew could never be the child's voice., "He ain't got no power."

He said, " I'll spit in his face" and he did, spit right in my face.

Being my apartment was too small after I started parenting I purchased a three bedroom home. I was dedicated to my children. Yes! They were my children. I had made a commitment, and I intended to keep it 'come hell or high water.' Sometimes I wondered what had I had gotten myself into, but I have never been a quitter.

Besides that, fact these precious kids were not only in my house, they were in my heart. I loved every one of them as if they were my own. God had loaned them to me to foster.

I was to nurture them, encourage them, and love them. People who didn't know me ,didn't know the difference. I dressed them ,kept up there appearance as if I had birthed them. I prepared nutritious meals for them.

Wanda would tell people when having a conversation about food, even when she became a teenager," my Mama wouldn't let us eat colored cereal " I had learned that the colored cereal just dyed the inside of the stomach. And anything that I didn't eat, I didn't give to my children. I didn't allow them to watch ungodly stuff on TV. I ordered movies from a company named Family Featured Films. (FFF). They were family oriented movies produced by a Christian company. There was no sex, no violence, and no vulgarities involved. I didn't have to screen anything, and they were very good movies.

Wanda was one of the girls that was so badly damaged from her environment, that a physiatrist told me if she didn't survive in my home, she would spend the rest of her life in a mental institution. But I knew better, because I knew the God who was going to deliver her.

I include this information because I assumed that this was the way it should be with every foster parent. But, I saw some things that were deplorable. It was just a job to some parents I knew. It was all about the money. The children were treated less than human. They looked the part of how some people would think a foster child should look. Only God knows what it takes to be a dedicated, nurturing, loving parent to these broken, damaged, and hurting children. And I can understand why other placements broke down. They didn't have what, or who it takes to empower them to get the job done.

After all, this was a ministry. The environment most of the children came from brought many spirits. But for twelve years God placed these children in my care so they could learn of His great love. They all were exposed to a different ,positive ,loving environment, by attending church. While in my care I planted seeds into these children's lives by taking them to church where they would be nourished with the word.

The Adoption

Wanda was one of three sisters who had been removed from their mother's care, or the lack of it. All of the parents were given the opportunity to meet the requirements to regain the custody of their children. If these requirements were not met, their rights were terminated. The mother of these children stopped showing up, even for visitation. Her rights were terminated. So, the children were eligible for adoption.

The State was encouraging, and even pushing adoption. They would continue to pay a small portion of the expense for the child's care.

There was another parent that had taken in one of Wanda's sisters. She was getting ready to move to Alabama. She was adopting Wanda's sister and she was asked to adopt Wanda. They was aware of the fact this lady was dying with cancer, but they would do anything to get these kids out of the system.

I had invested so much into Wanda, and I knew that somehow some way at some time, God was going to deliver her. So, I started procedures to adopt her. It was not long before Beatrice passed away in Alabama.

It was so very hard to watch what this child was going through. The worse of it started when she turned fourteen. This was no making of her own. She had begun her adolescence, and starting to become a young lady. It was so hard on her. She didn't know what was happening to hear. It was scary. She was the first of the two children I had, that was the most damaged. And the one that needed the most help. She is the one who gripped my heart, both emotionally, and physically.

The things I witnessed, and experienced with this child was unbelievable. But the more I witnessed her struggling ,the more I loved her, and prayed and cried out to God for her. It seemed as there was no hope of her getting any better.

It began to look like the physiatrist was right. But I failed to give up. Throughout her teenage years, from fourteen to eighteen, she was taken from one institution to another to be locked down like some wild animal. No matter where she went, no matter how far, and sometimes it was far from New Orleans, I was there for visitation.

There were times when it felt like I would have a stroke or a heart attack or just end up dead because of her devastating behavior. But I couldn't give her up. It was suggested by people who could foresee my destruction if I continued to keep her. But I just couldn't bring myself to abandon her. I would tell those that were concerned," I can't abandon her, she is not responsible for what happened to her as a child." When I would slightly consider it, I would listen to this song by Yolanda Adams, " What about the Children." The message in that song would cause me to cry, and cry, and cry.

Wanda would write about her agonizing experiences while she was locked down . It would tear my heart to pieces to read them. "Why was

God placing such burdens on me? I did not ask for this." Yet, I could not walk away from it.

She had made sixteen and was constantly running away She had gone to her mother's at the place where she was living before. One of my friends, a church members had seen her at the corner store where she lived, which was blocks from where Wanda's mom lived.

She told me she had to find her mom and find out why she didn't want her. The Social Worker was trying to find her, but to no avail. I was hoping it would work out with she and her mom, and maybe she would find some peace. But she displayed some behavior that caused her mom to call the social worker. I was preparing to go our Women's Conference in a few days I thought if I could get her there she could be delivered. She met me at my friend's home, and I invited her to come with me. She refused. The Social worker would have to find respite for her, or I couldn't go to conference. It was at this moment that I felt I couldn't go anymore. As much as I regretted having to do this, I had to give her up.

I was too overwhelmed. If they found a place for respite, that is where she would stay. She could never live with me again. At the last minute, a place was found for her to go for the weekend, and it felt like a ton was lifted from my shoulders.

I had seen those demonic spirits at work in so many ways. I kept gasoline in the back for the lawn mower, so when they were on the rampage, they announced that they would set the house on fire. At the same time, they were pouring the gas around the house. I had seen them grab six knives at one time threating anyone who came near them.

I witnessed them setting newspaper on fire under the bed and immediately called the fire department after smelling smoke. They tried to get my car into gear so it could roll down the driveway into the street. I have seen them outrun the Police, slip out of their handcuffs, and brag to the Police about it. I have seen them destroy a doctor's office in a rage. I have seen them pull the pictures from the wall of a therapist office and pull out the drawers of the desk throwing all of its contents to the floor, including the money that was inside. I have been present when it took three strong male attendants in the the facility to restrain them when they went on the rampage..

But I have seen the power of God cast them all out and their occupant who was Wanda became sane.

God's power is the only power that can cast out devils, tear down strong holds, and deliver those that are bound.

The Homecoming

After returning from the conference, I informed the social worker, that I was unable to continue to provide care for Wanda. They were upset at my decision, but I just didn't see any other way. I was charged with neglect because of this. That is what went on record, but I was still her legal mother. Every decision that was made concerning her they had to consult me.

There was no one in the program that was willing to take her. And there was no facility in the area with a bed available. So, they took her to West Monroe. I was broken hearted. That was a long ways, but if she had stayed long enough, I would have made my way there.

I stayed on my face before the Lord. I prayed, and I cried, day and night for her. God was taking me through the fire. Much sooner than I expected, God answered my prayers.

I got the news that they had a bed for her in a facility where she had previously resided on the West Bank. The name of the facility was Hope Heaven. There was something about the building on the outside that made it a little more tolerable to go and visit your loved ones. It looked just like a castle. It had pretty bright colors , pink and beige. But the atmosphere on the inside was less attractive. Not because of the appearance, but because of the reason for the residents being there. I jumped up and down when I found out that my baby was back so close to home; God had done it again.

I couldn't wait to go and visit her. When I entered her section and met with her, it was a sight for sore eyes. She was sitting there, calm as a cucumber, with all kinds of things to show me that she had done.

God had delivered her, Hallelujah!! Her birthday was two weeks away and I planned a visit to my home for her birthday. Since I did not have any more kids in my home. I had rented my house out. It was too big for me to keep up. I rented my house out to a lovely, big family and moved into a senior citizen residence. These were one bedroom apartments, and relatively small. Mr. Cooper was the nice man that managed it.

I picked Wanda up the Friday, a week before her birthday. I took her to the hairdresser and shopping for and outfit for her birthday. She looked so pretty, and didn't have any signs of illness By the time Sunday came, I was thinking, "She can live with me."

We had a great mother/ daughter weekend. I took her back on Sunday afternoon. She was to be discharged from State Custody by the end of that week which would be her birthday. The social workers responsibility was to provide an independent living residence for her after discharge .She had only a few days before we went to court for her discharge.

The social worker was not fond of Wanda at all because of her issues. Mrs. Joseph made the mistake of telling me, " I can't wait to get rid of Wanda, she is going to wind up dead, or either in jail."

"I told her she is not to speak that upon her because words have power. I'm speaking life upon her." She couldn't find a place for her, because she had waited until the last minute. She was going to stick her in the Covenant House. That is a place where people go when they are on the streets, and on drugs. I said no.

218

She then settled for the home where her youngest sister Sarah, lived with her dad. Custody of her younger sister was awarded to the dad when her mother's rights were terminated even though she had always lived with him. The only thing was that he was totally blind and on dialysis from the effects of diabetes. There was no supervision at all.

Wanda's little sister had been on her own since age eleven and had taken on the responsibility of helping to care for her dad. God had mercy on her, and watched over her. Today she is a wife and a mother taking good care of her children.

I said no to that proposition as well. When Mrs. Joseph ran out of oppositions trying to find a place for her, she sat down with us and explained, Wanda could live me, and she would make her a self-payee. They would pay for all of her school needs and other expenses It would be as if she was living in her own place.

Wanda stayed with me the night before, and we got to court a little late the next day. Judge Gray was officiating. We got settled, and she addressed Wanda. She started with, " Wanda, I understand that you're going to live with your mother. Now we can't pay you if you're living with her." When she finished I asked permission to speak. I explained that we had been told by Mrs. Joseph that she would be paid. Judge Gray was a little more than upset. It was kind of embarrassing. She asked " You mean to tell me you lied to this child? You take this child and her mother back there in that room and you straighten things out."

When she started trying to justify what she had done , I told Wanda , that's ok Wanda, you can live with me. You don't have to pay anything. We will make it by the grace of God. So, it was done. The one bedroom apartment I lived in could only accommodate only one resident . So, I went to Mr. Copper to give him notice that I had to move and why. He agreed that no one was allowed to live with me under my lease. So, we set out looking for a two bedroom apartment.

During the process of looking, Mr. Copper called me down to his office. He had found a clause in their rules pertaining to the lease. Wanda could live with me as long as she was in school. Not only that, but as long as she was in school she could earn up to four hundred thirty dollars a month without an increase in rent.

So, I bought a sleeper sofa for the living room, and she was officially living with me. One of the requirements from the state upon discharge of a child from custody was that they had to see a psychiatrist When I took Wanda to see one, he told her she was depressed, and he was prescribing medicine for it.

Wanda didn't mind boldly telling him, " I'm not depressed, and I'm not taking that junk. Y'all been keeping me on that junk for two years, and all it did was make me depressed ,and had me walking like a zombie. I got Jesus, and I don't need that." She had been diagnosed with bipolar disorder. And to that I can agree, but we were trusting in God for deliverance.

A Hunger for More

My mission with Foster Parenting was over, and I was ready for my next assignment. For some time, I was still experiencing loneliness and depression. I had this void in my heart . There was longing for more of God and what He had for me. Instead the devil was trying to strip me of what God had already given me. I was experiencing more church hurt, family hurt, within the church, and outside the church.

I was criticized by some about my singing. The first time I knew that my style of singing was different was when I was attending the Church on St. Claude Street, the one where I was physically attacked for taking my stand for truth.

The Prophet had told someone Sister Vegie was "Antiquated" Gosh! I didn't even know what that meant!" I found out the definition of antiquated meant outmoded or discredited by reason of age, old and no longer useful, popular, or accepted. Usually disapproving of things or ideas, old fashioned and no longer suitable for modern conditions.

Again, I was told that my voice was dominant . I was an "excellent leader" I was told, but too dominate to sing in a small group. One lady told me I needed to sit down and let the young people take over. I was about sixty- five then, I believe. Even Wanda and her cousin would laugh and mimic me singing.

Vergie Iglus

I was the worship leader for our Ladies Ministry and sometimes I would form groups when there was someone willing to participate. Once a question was asked during a meeting if there were any more suggestions as we were preparing for a Women's Conference, one young lady spoke up and said " Yes! I have one. I suggest we get somebody else to do the singing. Sis Vergie always do the singing. We need something fresh, and something new. We're tired of looking at the same old face."

"Owwww! That hurt! I called her by name and told her it's an awesome responsibility to lead worship for a conference. That sets the stage for the conference.

"You ain't the only one who can bring the spirit down Sister Vergie" she snapped. I was done. Let her do the leading of worship. I would be obliged to follow suit.

She was given the opportunity to do so, and prepared for it. The morning of the Conference she was nowhere to be found. She had overslept. I ended up leading the worship. Whenever we went out of town, the majority of the women went shopping and out to eat, and were out pretty late.

I was too glad to get to the Hotel, and that's where I stayed. I had to rest and be prayed up to be ready for the conference next the morning.

I remember the time I had been criticized, and made to feel less than capable of getting up before our group of Ladies to lead the worship.

The President of the Ladies Auxiliary had encouraged me to proceed with it anyway.

I felt so low in my spirit. I questioned whether God's approval was upon me. I knew that this desire that was deep down in me was beyond my control. It was more than just a desire; it was a need. It seemed I couldn't survive without fulfilling this need. It has always been there, and this is what I expressed when I later met with my superiors at church.

Can you imagine having a call on your life from God to preach, teach, or any type of ministry, and someone, tries to shut you down. It would be just like Jeremiah, when warned not to speak anymore in the name of the Lord.

"Sometimes I think, I won't speak about His message anymore I'll never speak in his name again." But then your message burns in my heart. It's like a fire deep inside my bones. I'm tired of holding it in. In fact, I can't. I hear many people whispering, "There is terror on every side! Bring charges against Jeremiah! Let's bring charges against him!" All my friends are waiting for me to slip. They are saying, "Perhaps he will be tricked into making a mistake. **Jeremiah 20:9-10 NIRV.**

We were in Baton Rouge for the Conference. It was about three o'clock in the morning when I had an encounter with God. My daughter-in-law and I were sharing a room this time. But she had chosen to visit her friends in another room and ended up staying the night.

The Lord woke me up and His presence filled that room. It was like lightning, and thunder and wind all at the same time. God spoke to me that morning. It felt like the time Jacob wrestled with the angel. He placed an anointing upon me that I couldn't shake it off if I had tried. The power and anointing didn't let up until it was time for me to get dressed for service.

I went down to the Conference room and when Sister Maddie turned it over to me for the worship the Holy Ghost took me over. The room was filled with His Glory. God had placed His approval on what He was doing through me. No one in the room could deny that it was Him who had taken over. There was no doubt that His presence was in that place. He uses whom He will.

After that time at Lady's prayer, or any function wherever we gathered I would open my Bible to read a scripture, and the Holy Spirit would take over. It seemed I could not contain myself. When I would lead in prayer , the Holy Spirit just would not let up.

There were complaints that "Sister Vergie go too long" I was still facing that "Saul spirit."

So, it was I who had to attempted to give it up, but the Ladies Auxiliary president, wouldn't allow it. There were some changes made that caused me to become less, and less involved with music. I still helped out at the other church with worship. This is where I would get my fulfillment I just had to sing. I did the proper thing and asked to meet with those that were in charge, and I got shot down. I was so depressed; I would deliberately go to church late and sit on the back seat. But I remained humble.

Wanda had moved back with me; my obligation was to her. I was not going to do anything to uproot her So, she never knew about my dilemma. But it was like the eagle stirring her nest. God was allowing me to feel the thorns.

I would drive along the street and cry and sing. The song I sang all the time was "Lord wherever you lead me I will go."

But it was more than a song. It was a prayer .It was me talking to God. I would sing and cry til it hurt. I felt the Lord calling me, pulling me. And I was answering His call. I knew it would not be long before I would leave New Orleans. I just didn't know by what means.

Seeking Refuge from the Storm

Wanda and I were building a brand new relationship. She didn't give an ounce of trouble. Prayers were being answered. She still had many issues to work out, but with the help of God, we would work them out together. I didn't judge her, or condemn her for anything, I just loved her unconditional . There was a major issue, she had to overcome that her biological Mom had instilled in her. I determined to "love" it out of her with the love of God.

225

We got her into Job Corp, and she attended faithfully, taking the bus to and from with no problem. I was helping a friend out at her daycare, near Canal Street where Wanda would get off the bus. She would walk there and ride home with me.

It had five days since her birthday, and she had come back to live with me. It was Friday. Hurricane Katrina was on the way, and we had to make it home in a hurry to ride out the Storm. We thought we were going to ride it out. But it became worse. We followed the news as it worsened.. The Mayor finally issued a mandatory evacuation. We thought it would be like the year before. When we went to Lafayette and back home the next day.

My oldest son had no intentions of leaving. I called and tried to convince him to leave. He told me , "I'm not going nowhere, every time we leave, nothing happens."

But somehow he failed to ease my mind. After the mandatory evacuation order, I called again and told him the rest of his family wanted to leave. He answered, "I'll be right here when they get back."

Kendrick had moved to Hartford, Connecticut, seven years before with Destiny and their daughter. He secured a job doing the same thing he was doing in New Orleans. His back got in such bad shape he was unable to work. Destiny just simply decided he was no more use to her, so she sent him back. She actually called me and told me "He can't work.

He no more good." I sent him a plane ticket, as a loan. He couldn't ride the bus, he said. His back was out."

Terry thought this would be his chance to have a relationship with his father. He was wrong. Kendrick was devastated over the breakup. He had to get spiritual help to help him through. He was so fragile. He stayed with me awhile and then moved in with his cousin Jack and his family. He had no choice but to attend church living with them.

In a few weeks he had spied out a sister in church with four children. Pretty soon they got married. It was a slap in the face to Terry. However, he stood up for him in his wedding, but there never was a relationship between him and his dad. Kendrick always choose someone else's children over his own flesh and blood. Terry still suffers from the effects of that rejection.

So, we picked up Kendrick and his new family. I was concerned about Lawrence and his family. Lawrence had mentioned that there was a gas problem as one of the excuses for not leaving. I planned to go back and take him some money for gas. When I called I got no answer. So, we headed out. Kendrick's wife's uncle had secured us a hotel in Beaumont, Texas.

It seemed we would never get to our destination. It took twelve hours to get to Lafayette. I was doing most of the driving and I was worn to a frazzle. I decided I would call around and find a Hotel in Lafayette instead of going all the way to Texas. Everywhere we called was full .

We were using cellphones which wasn't sufficient. I suggested we go by Miss Martha's to use a phone directory. When we called her, who answered the phone but Lawrence's daughter in-law, Agnes that was married to my grandson.

My son, the one who was not going anywhere had arrived ahead of us with his family. We couldn't find anything vacant, so we got back on the road and headed for Texas. Just before we got to the bridge going to Lake Charles Agnes called. Her grandmother had told her to tell us to turn around and come back.

Martha said "Miss Vergie is too old to be riding up and down the road. Thus, we ended up in Lafayette.!!

Miss Martha our Shelter from the Storm

There were seventeen people in Miss Martha's small house, but I was so grateful to have a shelter over my head. I was later inspired to write a song about this experience. My oldest son and his family of four, his oldest son and his family of three, Kendrick and his family of six, plus Miss Martha, and her grandson.

I honestly believed that we would be going back home in the next couple of days like we did last year. But as we sat and watched the devastating flood waters rise higher and higher, we knew that this was something that would not be over anytime soon.

We saw people on rooftops, and houses going under water .It was so depressing watching the disaster that was taking place. So many disasters developed from the initial one.

It was horrible! People that were not able to get out were trapped. Many lost their lives, and maybe some even lost their minds. So many believed that the storm would pass over like the one the previous year. So, they remained in their homes. Wherever the evacuees ended up there was help.

The Government had all kinds of resources set up for the evacuees. Therapists met us at some of the sights where we went to pick up supplies. They were prepared to help us deal with the effects of the disaster. I found myself counseling the counselor. My family had escaped the direct hit of the disastrous Hurricane, and the flood waters that followed, and I was grateful.

My heart went out to the poor people who were stuck in that awful situation and had no way out. The stories I heard in the following months from some of my friends would prick my heart. Everywhere I went I would testify of the goodness of God. No! I was not a victim; I was a victor.

We started searching for a church. Tricia called a few in the area. The one that responded was a little different from what we were used to. The van picked us up for the Midweek Service. We never went back after that night.

Vergie Iglus

We were informed of a church that was issuing supplies so went there. It was like a warehouse, anything and everything we needed was at that church.. Everyone was so friendly the Administrative Secretary, Debra was in charge of the operation. She invited us to church, and we went that Sunday, and we met Pastor Patrick. We were treated with so much kindness. That became our church home. Most of my family didn't stay very long, but I was there for six years.

I was still experiencing rejection, and hurt, for no reason. I felt alone, and depression began to creep in. Everything was piling up. Wanda, in her weak state of mind, turned on me, being led by negative influences. She had been so sweet since she had moved back in with me. Now she would look at me as if I was the devil himself. She would attack me with words that cut like a knife. I felt my heart swelling. And seemed it would drop out of my chest.

This is the point I had come to when I had to temporarily give Wanda up. But this time it was because she was being fed garbage about me. It was horrible. I threatened to leave her and go to Florida. But I weathered the storm one more day, and I stayed.

I was determined not to let any of this become known, but Miss Martha was aware of the agony I was suffering but not wanting to get involved, said nothing. But she was upset with all of them. She tried to console me as much as she could, but she remained neutral.

I tried to keep it from showing in church, but Pastor Patrick discerned it. He let me know that he did. The hurt that I was feeling showed. And he discerned where the source of hurt was coming from. He told me he had seen it and shared it with his wife.

He solicited different families, or individuals who had room to take some of us into their homes. My oldest son and his family were the first to go. I learned much later that they had been taken in by this nice couple, Brother Tom, and Sister Pricilla Cain. They had fixed up their used car lot for the family. Soon Walter and his family were able to buy a home where they are still living.

My youngest son and his family moved over to Baton Rouge, because of his job. Pastor Rick Almon found a place which was originally supposed to be for Wanda and I. We were still living with Miss Martha a month later when the second storm, Marie, hit and caused havoc in Texas, and roundabout.

That is the morning I woke up with the terrible onset of vertigo. The bed, the room, the whole house was spinning. I had never experienced anything like that before. I have had terrible experiences after that . I had to eventually give up driving on the interstate.

Debra from the church took Wanda and I into her townhouse, in the Meadows. Wanda registered with SLCC to obtain her GED. Debra made us welcome to anything in her home. We stayed with her at least two months while we looked for housing. Everything was full with all of the evacuees from New Orleans. Even the hotels were still jammed packed.

We finally found a place at Holy Family Apartment Complex. They had begun allowing folk into New Orleans to check on things and salvage anything that they could if anything had survived the flood.

I mentioned earlier that I had rented out my house and moved into the Senior Citizens Apartment. I was on the third floor . When I went to check it out, I found out that the water had not reached the third floor. However, the whole city stunk. We were asked to wear masks when we entered.

One of the sisters from the church, Sharon Carrol drove Wanda and I, along with her daughter April . April and Wanda were best friends by now. I needed someone to drive me back to pack up my things. Sister Debra asked if my family was going to help, but I told her they all had legitimate excuses why they couldn't. She offered to help me. Her sister had to get her things out the following Saturday. The Saturday after that she would go and help me.

I remember clearly it was two days before my birthday, October, fifteenth. I questioned whether someone would go and help me. Again, there were words shot at me that cut to my heart...I asked God " Why God are still putting me through the fire?" I cried for two days. My heart was broken. How much more could I take?

"Lord you know my heart. Why is it that every time I turn around I am being attacked from every side.?

I didn't know what to do. I was becoming despondent. For my birthday, Miss Martha took me to Piccadilly to comfort me. I made up my mind that day that I was not going to let anybody make me cry anymore. A promise hard to keep of course.

Debra and one other sister brought me to pack up my things. Pastor Patrick had her rent a U-Haul, and asked two of the brothers from church to assist in moving.

That Saturday, Pastor Patrick, along with Brent Lee and brother Carl went to New Orleans to help me move. He, along with the other two men, hauled my heavy furniture down three flights of stairs since the elevators were inoperable. We stopped on the way back and Pastor Patrick treated us all to lunch.

When we arrived at the apartment, he noticed how dirty the carpet was, he promised to send carpet cleaners. We had to take whatever we could get. Some of the folk that could offer us housing knew we were getting help from FEMA, and were taking advantage big time. The managers at Holy Family were one of them.

I will never forget the kindness, the support , and compassion of all of these kind folk who cared enough to go the second mile to help me and my family in our time of distress.

233

There's A Purpose For Your Pain

As you read my story you might think it is a fairy tale. But I have talked to many who have similar stories to tell.

It has been said that when you find fault with so many others, it's time to examine yourself! This statement is so true when you have the spirit of fault finding or have a negative attitude toward everything and everybody. The Bible tells us that "the heart is deceitful above all things, and beyond cure." **Jeremiah 17:9**. But He alone knows our hearts.

Once a family member had convinced another woman in the church that I was pure evil. I was the devil, I was no less than a witch. The lady called me and literally attacked me over the phone for treating this person so awful. There was no truth to it. It was ongoing accusations and lies that I had to bear. When I tried to defend myself, she interrupted me with " It's you Vergie, it's your fault we don't know our own hearts."

This was a person in a high position, someone who was supposed to be full of wisdom. But she had taken the word of someone else without even hearing my side. She had become my Judge and Jury.

I very calmly answered her. "Yes! You are right. We don't know our hearts. But God does. That is why when I pray every day, I ask God to search my heart and go deep down into the crevices and search it out. I ask Him to cleanse it, and destroy anything that doesn't belong there. And that's the way I live above condemnation." And I reminded her of the same identical situation going on in her family. She was hurt because of her personal family situation. She had shared with me. So calmly I asked her, "Is that your fault? Is it you instead of the other person?"

She suddenly remembered saying, You're right Vergie, you're right" I just didn't understand why I met so much opposition with the people who supposedly knew God as I did. There were those who judged me by what they were told about me, but they got to know me for themselves, and we became inseparable. God certainly allows us to experience certain things to teach us lessons.

I learned from my experiences of being lied about,, misjudged ,persecuted ,falsely accused, abused, never to judge a person by what another person says about them. I will love that person and get to know them for myself. And even if what the other person is so eager to say about them does not matter at all.   We are all sinners, saved by grace. Paul says it in **1 Corinthians 6:11,** And such were some of you.; but ye are sanctified, but ye are justified in the name of the Lord...

I adapted a habit from my present pastor, Derald Weber quite recently. He says when someone comes to him to bring a negative report, or some gossip, he holds up his hand and says woah. What he meant by that was don't go any further. Since then I do it all the time. I don't allow anyone to come to me with gossip about another person. I know how the results of it can effect that person. I have been a victim. The old folk used to say a dog that will bring a bone will carry a bone.

Reflecting, back, For a period of time when I was under a pastor that was a true Man of God. There were some circumstances that brought about some changes in the church. Some of the Saints didn't like these changes. They didn't approve of him since he was a man of a different race. He was the kindest, most humble and compassionate Man of God I had ever known.

This person would call me every day with some criticism about the Man of God. At first I just wouldn't answer. She would ask "You on the phone ? Get off the phone l wanna tell you something." I would literally start shaking when she would call. I know that sounds weird. But I did. I literally shook!

One day she called, and sputtered out some information that she had gotten from her husband who was on the board. She went on, " And did you know he did this, and did you know he did that, and did you know he's going to do that, now what do you think of that?"

I had just had enough. The buck stops here. I said to her, with boldness. "You know what I think , the Bible said touch not my anointed, and do my prophets no harm, and I'm scared to run down the Man of God".

She snapped back at me. "That's what's wrong with black folk now." I guess I blocked out the rest of it. She didn't realize that my heart was changed when I received the Holy Ghost. I didn't see colors. People are people. We as people of God are all one. No black, no white, no bound, no free, no Jew, no Greek. All different individuals, but all one in Him.

She never had any more use for me, but she did take one more shot at me. It was something she accused me of doing, but there was no truth in it at all. I am known for allowing people to have their say while I remain quiet. If you choose to chew me out, I'll let you finish. Jesus said to bless them that curse you.

I not only allowed her to say all of the ugly things she was saying, which was intended to really hurt me. But when she finished I apologized for the thing that never happened. That made her angry. She snapped "And you need to come off of that passive aggressive behavior." My! I couldn't win for losing. She stopped greeting, or speaking to me and tried to make sure I didn't get close enough to speak to her.

But there came a time I had to minister to her. God had prepared me for such a time as this.

A HIGHER CALLING

Everyone had gone their separate ways Wanda had settled down and become more like she was when she first came back home. I had gotten a job at Faith House through Counsel on Aging. I worked there until God was ready to move me. I met someone at the apartment complex that was working at Gulf Coast, ,Teaching Family Service, (TFS). I had

237

started training at the one in New Orleans, just to take one child ,Sharla, back into my home. My home was the only home in which she had survived.

I applied for the job at Gulf Coast and was hired. I was assigned to a client named Fred that no one else would stay with. They would go in the front door and out the back door, so to speak. Only one person stuck with him, and that was Mary, the one who evacuated him from New Orleans, and kept him with her family until he was taken into the Services at Gulf Coast.

Fred was not supposed to be in the program that I was working. SIL, meant Supervised Independent Living. The clients were supposed to be able to do everything for themselves, the worker was there only to supervise.

Fred could not do anything for himself. He was nonverbal and had many issues. It was very hard working with him. But I loved Fred. We worked seven on and seven off with him. I took him to church every Sunday, he loved it! He tried to speak, and came close to saying his name.

I worked with Fred for two years. He became unmanageable and had to be moved to another program that would better meet his needs. He was taken to a facility in Iota.

Wanda and I had moved from Holy Family to Willow Brook Apartments. I was out of work for the time being. I can't remember if

I was seeking another client, or if there just was none available at that time. But I know it was God's plan.

Brother Roy Bingham had called me one night from New Orleans. I would now go on Sunday's between our services, and do their worship service.   He was a fan of my "Antiquated " style of singing and had started a Church in Avondale, Louisiana.

I would now go on Sundays between our service, and do there praise service. I was fulfilled as the Lord would pour out His Spirit upon all of us.

Pastor Weber probably doesn't even remember, but that is where I met him for the first time. He was invited to speak for the church anniversary. I was on a program to sing that Sunday..

The night Brother Bingham called me to give me a prophesy he had always told me that my ministry was to the hurting. He told me that if I would record the songs I sang people would buy them. I knew that to record other artists songs I would have to get their permission, and/or obtain the copyrights.

Pastor Bingham actually checked all of this out. In his research, he found out it would cost a fortune to go into the Studio. So, I said, "Forget it"

But God had a "Perfect Plan.

"I sang on the praise team at the Church that I formerly attended in Lafayette and I did specials. My favorite artists were Babby Mason, before she changed her style, and Candi Staton. They were two of the most anointed artists I have ever heard. The anointing would just saturate me when I listened to, or sang their songs.

Back in New Orleans I would minister to different people on the phone. It was just automatic. Whatever people were going through they would discuss it with me I would burst out with a song that would minister to that need.

Even then it seemed supernatural. I had no plans to sing. Then I came upon the scripture that read, ""Let the message of Christ dwell among you richly as you teach and admonish one another with all wisdom through psalms, hymns, and Spiritual songs from the Spirit, singing to God with gratitude in your hearts" **Col.3:16, NIV."**

So, There it was, confirmation. It was as if the Word of God was coming alive right there in my mouth as it did when I opened my mouth to witness to others. One of my Sisters, Joan, who was going through something that I could certainly relate to would call me and say, " Sing to me." We both would get a real blessing right over the phone.

Another scripture reference is, "Speaking to one another with psalms, hymns, and songs from the Spirit. Sing and make music from your heart to the Lord," **Eph .5:19 NIV**.

I had always been told, "You have a beautiful voice " Now I began to hear, " Your singing is anointed." Yes, I knew! It's the anointing that breaks the yoke and will set people free from bondage. I didn't want just a pretty voice. I wanted hearts to be touched, and lives to be changed.

Wanda's Struggle

Wanda had really been living for God. She was involved with the youth and loved it. They showed her much love. I remember the time Pastor Patrick gave his daughter money to take her out to eat. She was doing well until one day she was waiting for the bus to come home from school. This young man, Jack began stalking her, and got her attention. He started coming around, and when I knew anything, she was pregnant.

She was remorseful over it. She thought enough to meet with Pastor Patrick with me present. He was so kind, and compassionate. He handled the situation with much wisdom. When he finished, she didn't feel like leaving the church. She was ready to start over. She had lost her testimony with someone who only cared about one thing and one thing only.

It turned out to be horrible for her and that precious little child. Satan had set a trap for her. He hounded her and treated her like mud. She made one more effort to make it right. She set up a meeting with the pastor so Jake could understand what God expected of her as a Christian.. The pastor explained to him that   she couldn't be unequally

241

yoked with a non-believer and if he wanted to continue a relationship with her, he needed to be in church. I was so proud of her.

Well! He promised to attend church with her every other Sunday. But business would continue as usual. He pressured her and tried to convince her that she had an obligation to him. She asked me to speak to him. His answer to me was that he knew people who 'had sex" and still attended church. I was feeding my pearls to swine. After the baby was born, it got uglier, and uglier. And the baby was right in the middle.

I saw her struggling to live for God, and I saw the devil pulling her in other direction. I prayed fervently for her. She had come so far. I had seen God deliver her from every kind of spirit you can name.

It was alleged that her Mom had violated her, and that spirit had possessed her. Because of this, no Foster Home was willing to keep her. How sad .

"It was not the so called "good" children that were in need of help. It was children like Wanda who needed the love that comes from the heart of someone willing to make the sacrifice

Jesus pointed out during His ministry on Earth, "It is not the healthy that need a Doctor, but the sick. **Read "Luke 5:31----Matt.9:12.**

At first, she took very good care of her little baby D'Jean. She never missed his bath time, his feeding, or his overall well-being. She was very meticulous about his clothes being on point. But Jack knew her weakness, and he played on her emotions. He juggled her heart like a toy on a string. She once told me that Jack was going to be the cause of her going back into an institution . I was so desperate to see her become free of this tormenting spirit that was overtaking her again.

You can't imagine the hell she suffered as a little girl. There are many ,many horrible things that could go into describing her life as a child, but I will spare you the details.

Some of it would be hard to believe anyway. But God had placed her in my care, and I was in it for the long haul. Some things only God and I are aware of because even she does not remember. God wiped it from her mind. Now she was caught up into something that was sucking her right back into a black hole.

She was running from place to place. Sometimes she took D'Jean with her, and other times she would leave him. Jack would drop her 'like a hot potato "and when it seemed she was moving on with her life, he would promise they would get back together again for the sake of the baby.

This went on, and on, and it was driving her crazy. She shared things with me and told me that he tried to convince her that she was obligated to him to perform the duties of a wife, just because she was his baby's mother. But he never had any intentions of getting married.

She finally gave up. She had been diagnosed with bipolar disorder since she was a child . Now all of the stress that was placed on her from this abusive relationship was too overwhelming for her. She became very angry, and aggressive. There was physical, and verbal activity going on with the both of them in the presence of the baby.

By this time D'Jean was spending most of the time with his Grandma Joyce. But he spent every **Saturday Night,** with me since he was born so he could go to church. Plus, my home was considered his second home. He had his clothes, his toys, his room all at my home. For eight years, whenever I was in church, there he was.

The Anointing Falls

After my job ended at Gulf Coast with Fred, I was home in the morning. This too, was a part of God's plan. He was surely directing my steps. Instead of getting up to go to work every day, I had more time to spend with God. I would grab my Bible to read my scriptures. Every chapter I read, turned into a song. I knew God was calling me to a higher calling.

I remember when I was facing persecution in New Orleans, I learned to encourage myself in the Lord. That is what inspired one of my songs, *"God's Perfect Plan"* and the title of this book. I imagined God with great big hands. He held them out and I climbed up into them. Now! No one can touch me. Not with their harsh words, not with their lies, or accusations. No way, I was in His hands and He would protect me. There were times when I would be riding in my car, the power of God would sweep over me, and a song would be born.

The first song God gave me was " *I'm Not Looking Back.*" I had thought that surely this disastrous event we had experienced with Katrina would bring about a change in family relationships. But this had not happened. Things had not changed, not even when my son had died. I was slipping back into depression and that was the last thing I wanted to happen to me.

In spite of all the hurt I suffered of which I will spare the details I was determined to keep my heart clean and remain humble before the Lord. That's the only way He could use me. And I wanted to please Him in every way.

I decided I was going to escape slipping back into the dark pit of depression. I needed to let go of the past completely. Whatever happened, or didn't happen in New Orleans, before the depressing hurricane, its aftereffects, and all of the hurt, the pain, rejections, and disappointments, in the past, and up until the present, it all had to go. No looking back.

Thus, the song was born. " *I'm Not Going to Look Back*". As I **read Psalms 139**, I knew the Lord was speaking to me." All the times I had been falsely accused, lied on ,talked about, only God knew me. I said to the, "Lord, I have been puzzled. I have tried to serve you with my whole heart. Since I gave you my life, I've been sold out. I have humbled myself to those that are in authority. Yet , I'm misunderstood, accused

,and despised. But you know me Lord, and that song," Nobody Knows Me Like You "was birthed.

Every song I wrote was not me writing. Sometimes at two, or four o'clock in the morning, the awesome power of God would pull me out of my sleep, and shower me with His presence, and He would give me a song. One after the other.

My daughter would be sleeping across the hall in her room. The anointing would fall on me and she would yell," Maaaa! I'm trying to sleep." I had no control over what was going on inside of me, these songs were conceived and birthed. I never had to write them down for the sake of remembering them. They were imbedded in my heart. I felt pain at times, as if they were labor pains.

Once I held my stomach and asked the Lord, "Lord, What are you doing?" I remember when God gave me the song, "Send Me," I was on my way to Women and Children's Hospital with Wanda. I couldn't wait until she got out of the car. I was birthing another song.

I had this heavy burden for lost souls. I wanted so desperately to reach out to everyone I could for the kingdom. So, I sought the face of the Lord one day while in prayer. I would ask the Lord, Lord, what will you have me do? He said "Lift up your eyes towards the Harvest. Tell me my Child, what do you see.?

" I said Lord, I'll labor for you, here I am , Oh Lord! Send Me."

The Holy Ghost had inspired me to write ten songs. It was as if I was in a daze, or a bubble . I felt I was in the safety of His arms.   I was being driven by some supernatural force. It was like an out of body experience. God gave me the rhythm to every song. I recorded them on a cassette. When I finished, I made an appointment with Pastor Patrick. I almost ran to his office with my songs, and with the rhythm to all of them.

He had no idea what it was about when I asked for the appointment. I hesitate to say the Lord told me this or that, like I hear a lot from some other people. The Lord tells them every single thing. Not judging, but it just doesn't happen with me. But if God ever spoke to me, He was speaking to me now. He told go to the studio and record these songs.

I told Pastor Patrick ." I'm not asking for anything. I just want you to listen to something." I played the cassette and he listened to it and said he was impressed. He loved my songs.

I told him I was going to the studio and record. Not having one clue where to start, what to do, nothing. But I knew I was going to do it. Then he told me to talk to Jimmy Mouton, that he could point me to someone that could help.

Jimmy gave me the information for a guy that he worked with. He was the best around these parts. People came all the way from other parts of the country to record with him. His name was Michael Lockett, he is totally blind. He and Jimmy traveled internationally with their band. The good news is that his studio was less than three miles from me.

Tried as I may, I couldn't catch up with Mike. He is still that busy Man, traveling all over the country. So, someone told me about another studio not too far from me. I was really anxious to get these songs recorded and get them out to the public. More so, to get the message out to the hurting, the broken and the hopeless.

In a hurry, I contacted this producer Joseph and he gladly worked out a plan to record my songs. I had to come up with five hundred dollars to start. He would shave it off by the hour. That turned out to be a very disappointing experience.

Finding a Studio

Joe would set a time for me to get to the Studio. That is when the hour started. He arrived late and fiddled around in the front of his studio. He displayed different merchandise he displayed. Then when he finally came to the back he would play with his computer as if he was looking for something and couldn't find it. This was time taken off the five hundred dollars.

I was on pin and needles. I literally wanted to jump out of my seat. He was counting all that time to shave off the five hundred.. I was not as anxious about the money as I was about getting my songs recorded.

We didn't get one thing done. Before I knew it, he was shutting down his studio for a period of time, and had moved to a new location on Moss , Street. When he was up and going, he never got in touch with me. I hunted him down and found out where the new studio was located. He wouldn't answer the phone or return my calls. I found him in the studio one day, went in and asked for him. He just simply would not come to the front.

A couple of years after I recorded my music I ran into him. He was playing music at his mother's church, at that time. I received a lot of invitations for places to sing. When I walked in his eyes enlarged. I didn't show any signs that I remembered anything. I had long forgiven him and moved on.

I did sell him a CD. But I got absolutely nothing for my five hundred dollars, Nothing!! I hear he's a preacher now!

Someone else put me in touch with another young man named Michael Lollis. They were a well-known family of recording artists from Abbeville, Louisiana. They did their recordings in their church. I was desperate to get my music recorded, so I contacted Michael Lollis and he agreed to record my music in the church. I drove to Abbeville and we did a couple of songs, but I wasn't satisfied with the quality of the music, because it was not a padded studio.

Back to the drawing board! Michael had the greatest attitude about it, and played base on all of my projects. Like my son William, he could make a base talk.. Whoever has my CDS, or heard my music can testify to that.

I contacted Jimmy Mouton again and he nailed down Michael Lockett. The first producer, set up an appointment, and escorted me to his studio.

At last! We began our project and Mike never asked for a penny up front.! We layed the tracks and we were on our way.

Part of the praise team from my church, Carman George, Karen Derise, Jimmy Nugent, Anjelle Andrews, and Dustin Gibson did the background for my first CD, " *Shelter From The Storm's.* "

Mike set up a payment plan just for me. The Lord had given me favor with a top notch producer, and the studio was only two and a half miles away, and I didn't have the burden of how I would finance the project.

As soon as I received my first order of CDs, they were sold, and I paid Mike off. I had passed another test. Losing five hundred dollars was not going to make me give up. God had ordered my steps once again.

One of the perks to all of this is that my producer, Mike Lockett began attending church with me. He was inspired by my music. He would come down to the studio humming tunes that we were recording. He would tell me, "Ms. Verge, that song has been in my spirit all Night " He has never stopped attending church since then.

Surely God had a "Perfect Plan"

When this project of mine was completed, something happened. It was as if the whole world had been shut off and I had been shut in with God. I would listen to the songs and all the hurt, all the pain. I was still experiencing rejection from family members, none of it mattered anymore. God had used this music, these song, to bring a complete healing to my life.

He confirmed it over and over again. Everyone from far and near, whoever had access to my CDs , called or spoke to me in person to let me know that they were being blessed by my music. I never expected to receive phone calls from preachers from different states, telling me how they were being blessed.

Pastor Harry, from Mississippi , called to say he was listening to my CD, and wanted to know if I really wrote the songs. He had been preaching for fifty-four years, and now was on internet radio. He would be "playing my music, and it would go all over the world."

God had given me these songs for a dual purpose, to complete my healing, and to bless many others. He had blessed me, to be a blessing.

After my first and second projects, I traveled a lot throughout the state of Louisiana, and Florida. I met more than one person who told me that they had to get up in the middle of the night to put my music on.

My music was being played on the local radio stations, and on twenty-four hour internet radio. This did not cause me to be lifted up, or feel exalted. It was the opposite with me. I felt really humbled, and still give all the glory to God.

Pastor Patrick told me he was one of my biggest fans. He loved my music, and was very supportive. After the first CD was completed, "Shelter From The Storms" He allowed me to put on a concert at the church.

When someone gave me a compliment, and I receive many, I dared not take the credit. I quickly admit that it was not I but the Holy Ghost that was working through me. It amazed me, every time I listened to one of the songs how everything fell in place. I knew that in my flesh, I had not the wisdom nor knowledge to put it together. But it ministered to me every time. They were my comfort.

My Next Mission

Wanda had begun going off for weeks at a time, leaving D'Jean. with his paternal grandmother to care for him. He missed his mom something terrible. He had the worst kind of eczema. He slept with me two-thirds of the time, including every single week-end and attended church with me. At night it was pitiful. No matter what we used, it didn't seem to help . He could not sleep for the terrible itch. I felt it was unreal that a little baby had to scratch himself that way. The scales that resembled toad frogs would bleed as he scratched. We put gloves on his hands to try and protect him. My heart went out to him. I stayed awake most of the night, rubbing his wounds so that he could get some sleep. I rubbed, and I prayed. I prayed and I rubbed.

Then God in His great mercy, heard, and answered my prayers. He completely healed that baby's body of that awful plague. God had cleared his little body just as He did the lepers.

He began to have faith in God from that moment. He was about two years old when he began grieving for his mother. It was really pitiful. He was so precious. so innocent, so handsome, so smart, and sweet. But he was depressed.

I had developed this tremendous burden for those that are depressed. I had gone through it with William. I had fallen into a state of depression after he died. I remember walking through the Lake Forest Mall soon after I had found my way back to trust in God after my son died.

I saw a young man sitting on a bench with his head down in his hands. I ran to him and asked if he was ok. I was ready to minister to him, and anyone I could find to introduce them to the one who could deliver them from their depression. I was not yet delivered ,but I knew it would come . I knew that God could and He would. deliver me. I realized that God was bringing me through these fiery trials for such a time as this.

But why, Oh, why? Had God chosen me to witness the kind of suffering that this precious child would suffer. It was torture. No human being, especially a child who did not come into the world of their own accord.

As I previously mentioned ,in the case of Terry being abandoned by his father, children are a gift from God. He does not punish them, no matter by what the circumstances of their coming into the world.

There is no such thing as an illegitimate baby/child. A child should be loved, and they should be able to feel the love. They need to be cuddled ,and hugged. They need to be held, and rocked . They need to be listened to, and to be heard.

I saw this baby as a crawler at the feet of his mother being rejected. The mother had been so damaged; it was being spewed out upon this child. There is a true saying ,"Hurting People, hurt People." Surly she didn't know what she was doing. A mother in her right mind , would never tell her baby while crawling around her feet , longing to be picked up and held, "get out the way, before I kick you in the mouth." That's when I knew that I needed to do what I had to do to protect him.   I am being very transparent in writing of these events. I truly hope that some Mother or Father reading this will realize the damage that is caused to a child who does not know the love of their parents.

Yes! D' Jean heard it with his own ears, " I don't want him, I didn't have him by myself." He was exposed to much violence, vulgarities, physical altercations, dirty rap music, from both parents and others.

One day he got permission from his mother to come and visit her. Yes, he had to get permission . She got upset about something, threw him out the door, pushing him out with dirty words to follow, and slammed the door behind him?

He came as far as the car where I had parked to drop him off. He sadly said," I'm not leaving!". She reluctantly let him back in. That scene was etched into my mind for a long time. My heart was raw. I cried for a week, every time I thought of it.

That baby slept in my arms month after month, weeping, and crying for his mother. He refused to sleep in "his" room. He needed the comfort that he thought only I could offer him. But I knew that only God could give him lasting comfort.

One of the most heartbreaking scenes I have ever witnessed with him was the night I heard him wailing in the next room. I went to him and he was curled up on the floor in the dark crying," Mameeee! Where you at?" He was only three years old. He had not heard from her in a long time. My heart could hardly survive what he was suffering.

I witnessed those same spirits that I had witnessed in his mother trying to take him over. At night he would struggle, and make strange noises. But I had power over those demonic spirits, and they could not stay . I prayed for him all through the night. And I held him close.

He would tell me, "Let's snuggle " He said I was the only one that hugged him. I tickled him and made him laugh! That would take his mind off of his mom for a little while. There were times he longed for her so bad he would insist on his grandmother Joyce or myself drive him by her apartment to see if she was at home. He would be so disappointed when she was not there.

I have heard tragic stories of how mothers and occasionally fathers take the lives of their children some by drowning, shooting, or by some other method. I refused to believe that these parents would perform such actions if they were in the right frame of mind. I had to come to this conclusion to avoid having resentment or bitterness towards Wanda.

I had to believe that this was all for the good of D'Jean. This was God protecting him. I told myself that she really did love him, but was unable to parent him. I had always told him that she loved him, and that God was working on her. He would fix her, and she would come back to him.

Some people have a tendency to poison the mind of a child, when they are going through the pain of rejection, and abandonment. That is like adding fuel to the fire. No matter how bad it was, I have always built that parent up in the eyes of the child. It is not the will of God to teach hatred and resentment under any circumstances. We teach love, and pray, pray, pray!

Periodically he would ask me, "Where is Mommie, is she fixed yet"? *What did he do to deserve this God?* I felt so helpless. I would have done anything within my power to ease his pain.

D'Jean's Ongoing Care

At the age of four D'Jean refused to sleep in his bed. Rather he slept with me for the next four and a half years. We never failed to pray together and fall asleep by my music. His favorite song was, *"Miracle Worker"* He had named it, *"Miracle in My Life"* He would request it to be played. "Maw Maw, I wanna hear *'Miracle In My Life.'*

Surely, indeed he needed a miracle in his life. He was in school , but couldn't focus. He had too much on his little shoulders, grieving for his mom. In spite of that, he had trouble reading, he had a mild case of dyslexia.

It's sad that caregivers don't understand the effect it has on a child when they are already struggling with any kind of task or problem. The last thing they need is to be rebuked, and criticized, and made to feel you are unworthy. I saw D'Jean in this state. He was constantly being told. "You can't read, you can't read."

I am writing this, and everything else I pen in this book hoping that someone who means well, like D'Jean's caregivers, will glean something from my experiences and be helped in some way.

The child who feels unloved, unwanted, rejected, and abandoned needs an abundance of love and hugs, and encouragement. If a parent or a caregiver is unable to provide this then they should be encouraged to solicit that part from someone who can, such as a tutor., or a Christian counselor.

Sometime in the modern school system homework can be challenging especially when raising grandchildren. But there should never be a lack of love and encouragement . I would have taken my heart out, and given it to D'Jean if I could have.

I saw D'Jean walking one day with his nose to the ground. His neck looked like a crane's neck. It was a pitiful sight. He was saying, " I hate school, I can't read, I hate school!" I went to him and I said " Hold your head up, and don't ever let me see it down again. you can read. You have a little dyslexia, but that does not mean you are dumb. It means you're smart."

I gathered him around the table, got out the computer, and we looked up Dyslexia, and some people who had it. Such as Albert Einstein's a genius, and they shared the same birthday.

From that point on, his countenance changed. His head lifted , he went around repeating, "I'm smart, I'm smart!" Maw, Maw, I'm glad I have dyslexia , I'm smart." In fact, he became really cocky, and I loved it. Before that day, and until this day, I always tell him he's one of the smartest little boys I know. And he is.

When dealing with the feelings of others, especially children ask God for wisdom, He will give it to you. He did it for me!   There is so much power in words. Words can make or break a person. I have been in the presence of parents who curse their children as a way of life. The Bible teaches us how to use our words. We must take time before we speak.

The Bible tell us, a soft answer turns away wrath. "Be slow to speak, swift to hear, slow to wrath." **James 1:19.**

Take time to be kind. Go out your way to encourage a child. I hope I never have to witness what I did with the two little boys, Terry and D'Jean .

Children are people too!

'Wanda 'had been gone for about four months when I heard from her. She was requesting to move back in with me. I was literally shaking when I agreed to allow her to come back, but I would remain true to my word. "I will do anything within my power to take away his pain."

I had to look to God for strength. I had endured too much stress in this lifetime, but this was an opportunity for D'Jean to spend time with his mom and I was not going to stand in the way. When I found out she was pregnant, I was still willing to work it out for D'Jean's sake. But an incident occurred that caused me to change my mind. I got her into a Women's Shelter and within one month was in her own apartment. For the first time she was on her own.

By this time, I had produced my second CD, *"The Finishing Line."* I began to run into more opposition. There had been no discussion concerning my music before , as all of the specials I had sung up until now had been traditional. Again, I didn't understand the why's of certain things. Since I was totally inspired to write these songs, I didn't know anything about the rules and regulations of certain churches.

When I came from my New Orleans church, I came from an entirely different, musical background. We sang songs from all of the mass choirs,. We also sang Donald Lawrence, John P Kee, etc., many of which I had the lead.

It was strictly traditional. I had never heard, or sung contemporary music. I never attended a music school. All I had ever known was the anointing.

When I started attending this new church in Lafayette the music was very different, but it was anointed. Though it took some getting used to. I was blessed to be a part of that wonderful ministry for six-years.

But God had another Plan.

The first time I heard of "Vertical, versus horizontal," was after my second CD. And I learned about "Finding your own ministry " I learned there are different kinds of churches.

One of them is classified as a Contemporary Church where you sing up to God, but otherwise, it's to yourself. With my style, I was told by only one person I would better fit in the church where I came from in New Orleans.

I was invited to many churches some repeatedly whose congregation declared to be blessed by my ministry. And that is what is is all about. So, when I met this music minister at an event in Opelousas, Louisiana,

I accepted his invitation to minister at his church in song. After my first visit the Pastor invited me to come on a regular basis, every fourth Sunday to minister.

This was a full gospel church and it was right near me. They had three services on Sundays. Julian, and I were there, for the services He went to toddler church. My mind was very clear when I accepted the invitation. I thought, " *Maybe I have found my ministry.*"

I would still make it to the service at my church, but a little late. I was in a struggle. I had this need to be fulfilled in the ministry that I knew God had given me. It was not a need to be heard. This desire, this fire, that was burning down in me was a yearning in my soul to get songs heard by those who were grieving, and hurting, lonely , and depressed. I wanted them to know that there was a way out.

I could not just sit in one place and hold my peace. It would lead right back to my state of depression. This was a God thing. It had nothing to do with me. I contacted my pastor and requested his blessings in my decision to depart so I could walk in my calling.

He made a suggestion, but to follow it meant leaving Lafayette. It was only one of the options I had, So, I remained at the church where I was singing. It was not at all even close to what God expects His church to be.

Everyone was super friendly and loving, but from the pulpit to the front door, there were zero standards. There were other things going on that I knew were definitely not in the will of God. But I tried to find ways to justify my reason for being there. Maybe God had planted me here for a season. I would be a light in the midst of darkness.

When the music minister asked me to do a lead with the choir, and they dressed in their regular attire, tight jeans and shirts. I wore my jean skirt. It was like trying to fit a round peg into a square hole. I got fidgety every time the pastor would give the invitation to those that were in the congregation.

No! He didn't make an altar call. He asked if there was anyone in the congregation that was not saved. Someone would raise their hand and they were instructed to repeat after him. He would then tell them, "Now you are saved, now you are sanctified, now you're in the Kingdom of God" That was It. I squirmed in my seat, more, and more.

After a couple of months after going there, I never heard him preach a message on salvation, or repentance ,baptism , and the in-filling of the Holy Ghost .

I couldn't take it any longer. I called the pastor and asked him if and when they baptized, and how did they baptize. He answered "Ms. Vergie, we do it all. We baptize in the Name of the Father, Son, and Holy Ghost, and in the name of Jesus.

He went on to tell me that they had people there from all kinds of backgrounds, and he didn't want to offend anyone. I then explained to him the significance of being baptized in the name of Jesus. I never knew if that was my mission there, or if it made any kind of impact at all. I was a little lost. I was not satisfied ,but I didn't blame it on anybody

Again, I was like a sheep without a Shepherd.   I had learned that when things don't seem to be going in the directions I think they should go, I stop and reflect on **Romans 8:28**   And we know that all things work together for the good of those who love Him, and are called according to his purpose."

I loved Him, and I was called by Him, for His purpose. Again, it was like the eagle stirring her nest. God makes it very plain that in order to be in fellowship with Him, we must be in one accord.   The church that Christ   designed did not tiptoe around feelings of those who were uncomfortable with his word or were offended with its doctrine. He said offences would come. **Amos 3 :3--** Can two walk together, except they be agreed?

Also, in the Book of **Philippians 3:15-16,** We learn, Let us therefore, as many as be perfect, be thus minded: and if in anything ye be otherwise minded, God shall reveal even this unto you. Nevertheless, whereto we have already attained, let us walk by the same rule, let us mind the same thing .

Be ye not unequally yoked together with unbelievers: for what fellowship hath righteousness with unrighteousness? And what communion hath light with darkness? And what concord hath Christ with Belial? Or what part hath he that believeth with an infidel? And

Vergie Iglus

what agreement hath the temple of God with idols? For ye are the temple of the living God; as God hath said, I will dwell in them, and walk in them; and I will be their God, and they shall be my people.

Wherefore come out from among them, and be ye separate, saith the Lord, and touch not the unclean thing; and I will receive you. And will be a Father unto you, and ye shall be my sons and daughters, saith the Lord Almighty...**2 Corinthians 6:14- 18.**

They were believers. I just didn't believe what they believed. What I had attained of the Word of God, and His truth, was forever etched in my heart. The only direction I desired to go was forward, not backwards.

The End of An Era

I started my search for a church where I could be among the people of God. A church where the word was being expounded the way Jesus had commanded it to be preached. I was looking for a church where the leadership was concerned about soul-winning, and not just about numbers.

A pastor is supposed to play the role of a Shepherd. That's an awesome responsibility. God holds the Shepherd responsible for souls that are lost because of their lack of telling them the truth.

"Woe be unto the pastors that destroy and scatter the sheep of my pasture! saith the Lord. Therefore, thus saith the Lord God of Israel

264

against the pastors that feed my people; Ye have scattered my flock, and driven them away, and have not visited them: behold, I will visit upon you the evil of your doings, saith the Lord. And I will gather the remnant of my flock out of all countries whither I have driven them, and will bring them again to their folds; and they shall be fruitful and increase. And I will set up shepherds over them which shall feed them: and they shall fear no more, nor be dismayed, neither shall they be lacking, saith the Lord. **Jeremiah 23:1-4 .**

THAT'S SCARY!

Read Ezekiel: Chapter 34.

I had somewhat of a relationship with Wanda still trying to reach out to her on behalf of D'Jean. Everywhere I went he was there with me. Wanda was aware of my pursuit of a church home. We were communicating on a regular basis. One day when we were talking she said out of the blue. "We got to find us a church."

" Oh! Happy Days!

I had been thinking in the back of my mind about this church that I had been told about. Pastor John Cupit had called me after the flooding from Hurricane Katrina, to check on my family. He asked whether we had found a church, and kind of told us to go visit the Church that was located pass the mall. I told him we were going to another church.

He said, " That's okay too, but when you get a chance, go visit that one past the Acadiana Mall.

"Pastor Weber the reason I had not visited before was due to its location." I was looking for something closer to home and this seemed it would be like driving to another city. I lived one mile from the former one, but the minute Wanda said ,"We got to find us a Church." The Pentecostals Of Lafayette " was the first church that popped into my mind.

We visited the next Sunday. During the worship service, I looked over at Wanda and told her, "This is it!" I had found where God had been leading me to, step, by step. It wasn't so much of what I heard in that short period of time that I was there., it was what I felt. It had only been a minute. I had hardly sat down. It was like trying on several pairs of shoes and knowing when the right ones fit.

I had arrived at my destination. I found a very unique church, with very unique leaders. The teaching and the preaching of the word was phenomenal by Pastor Weber, and First Lady Karen Weber. I was astonished by the amount of teaching that was focused on making sure that everyone who came through the doors, and had a serious desire to live for God; had a firm foundation.

Love is taught and shown by our leaders. They have a heart for children, which is my heart. I had brought a broken little boy there and he felt the love from everyone. I saw Pastor Weber get on his knees to show this little boy how much he cared about him. I saw Sis Weber, stoop down to his level to take a picture with him.

That's love! I have never been a part of a church where the pastor places a dollar in a birthday card for every single child for their birthday. Maybe so. I just didn't know about it.

YES! This was Home. I had decided that when I did find a church it would just be a sanctuary for my soul. I would be where I could be fed and worship and praise God in the beauty of His Holiness.

I was never going to let anyone know that I sang. It had turned out to be too complicated trying to sing in certain churches. The desire was still there. The fire still burned, and in some cases I've had to learn the hard way "It's better to be asked up than to be asked down. I was invited to several churches, and different events to sing, and felt the liberty. All I wanted to do was get the message out that was in my music. Someone always heard me and invited me to different events.

I was standing in Marvel's Thrift Shop singing but I wasn't aware I was being videotaped by Eric Treiul , the Minister for Chi Alpha. He had posted it on Facebook having obtained my information from Marvel and invited me to come and minister to the UL Students. It was at the little House/Church, called "Meal with a Message."

I also enjoyed the times I got to minister at the Jockey Lot, a large flea market ,where people came from many different places to shop. It was about two months later while at the Jockey Lot that Brady Borel, his wife Lauren and son Braydon came walking through and discovered me playing, and singing.

The Cat was out of the box!

Brother Brady passed the news on to Pastor and Sister Weber. Pastor Weber asked me to do a Special. The first time I sang was a couple of weeks later, on Grandparents Day. I became a member of the choir for a brief period of time until physical circumstances caused me to discontinue.

I sat next to my friends Rhonda and Terry Jennings for two months and they didn't even know. After singing that Sunday they invited me to the nursing home to sing for the residents. This was truly a blessing to go to the six nursing homes that were serviced by our church, TPOL. It was such a blessing to see them being blessed.

'Wanda' was still in a struggle to live for God. She was determined, and she fought, but there were always outside influences calling her. She got rebaptized at TPOL and she and I and D'Jean, were together in church for a while..

Then it was on again, off again with his emotions. The enemy was out to destroy the both of us, one way or the other. The Bible tells us the devil comes to "Kill, steal, and destroy." "I will never, ever forget the night that he tried to take us both out through a dream.

I was having a nightmare. D'Jean was sleeping in my arms. In the dream, a bad guy was chasing me. I ran for my life. He caught up with me, and I fought him with all I had. I got my hands around his neck and I squeezed with all the strength I had. The choking sound that D'Jean was making, in real life, woke me up. If the devil had succeeded we both would have been gone today.

There is no way would I have survived a tragedy of that sort. I would not have wanted to live. When I woke up and released him, he asked, " Maw Maw, why were you chocking me?"

You can't imagine the sorrow, the heaviness, the burden that I carried at that moment. I wrapped him in my arms and assured him that I would never ever hurt him. All I longed to do was protect him.

This incident was one I didn't want to remember. Every time it came to my mind, I would break down. I remember trying to share it with Pastor Weber months later, but it was too much. I became emotional. I praise my God for his mercy upon me that night.

D'Jean got baptized in the precious name of Jesus when he was nine years old. While searching for a church home, one of the churches I visited was a small church a few streets from where I lived. There I met Brenda Narcisse. A few years later God directed me to the place where she was visiting with her mother-in-law.

Little did I know that she was in the position of a " sheep without a Shepherd. " I invited her to our upcoming Family and Friends day at the church, which was now my home, The Pentecostals of Lafayette. She has been there ever since, faithfully serving the Lord.

The following is Brenda Narcisses' personal testimony:

Vergie Iglus

I got married in 1973 and became pregnant. My Mom died that same Year, and I thought it was the right thing to do. My husband beat me for no reason at all. He was unfaithful and contracted a disease, that he passed on to me. After my Son was born, I had to remain in the hospital two weeks in isolation because of this. We had three other children together, two boys and a girl. I had to walk on eggshells to him .At first we lived with his parents and he still beat me. One night I didn't want to go by his Moms. He threatened me and I jumped out of the car and ran in the cane field. He tried to run over me, but God stopped the car. It would not move, even, though the ground was dry .God is so good.

We moved to New Iberia, Louisiana, and lived on a farm. We raised chickens and hogs. I remember when my last baby was three Months old, I prayed to god to take me out of that marriage. I left and went to live with my sister because I just couldn't take anymore. He kept coming around trying to get me to reunite with him. I refused I finally left my sisters and went to Bossier city to live with my Brother. He found his way there .He tried to convince me to come with him.

When I refuses, he threatened me again. He told me that he was going to buy a pistol, and when I got back to new Iberia, he was going to pistol whip me and then shoot me. I pointed up to Heaven and told him "that's what you say, but that's not what God says,"

When I went back to New Iberia, he came to my sister's house and ,broke the glass on the door and shot my friend twice in the back. The bullet went right through her body, and never touched her spine. After he shot the second shot, the gun jammed. He came in the House and couldn't, find me and my children, or the lady he had shot. I had dragged the Lady in the closet with myself and my Children. That closet was so small. Only God! He is a hiding place.

In 1995 I was baptized in Jesus Name and two years later received the gift of the Holy Ghost. I was so hungry for God . I wanted to live for Him with all my being.

Because I wanted to be real, I suffered much Church hurt. The hurt came from Pastors, Pastors Wives, and other Sisters. I witnessed preachers practicing witchcraft, gambling, and Saints watching X-rated movies.

My deepest hurt came from my husband and family.
I tried to live the life that I knew God wanted to live, a life of Holiness. After the fourth Church failed I was seeking Gods directions, when He lead me to TPOL. I went as a guest by Miss Vergie, and I found what I was looking for, in leadership, and in the family of God.
I'm determined to live my life for Him.

Conclusion

God has not, and will not start a work that He won't finish. "Being confident of this very thing, that he which hath begun a good work in you will perform it until the day of Jesus Christ:" **Philippians 1:6.**

271

I don't understand why God chose this path for me. Maybe because He knew He could trust me. There were times when I felt like throwing in the towel ,but there was always someone He had placed in my life to stand in the gap for. I could not let them down, no matter what! My needs, my wants, my desires did not matter. I have always chosen to live my life, first for Christ, and then for others.

One thing I do know. God will never, never fail you. No matter what you go through. He's right there holding your hand. He went with me through my abusive, marriage, church hurt and persecution, The tragic death of my son, family hurts and rejection all for the purpose that he had designed for me.

I have been through the fire, but I was not burned. I didn't drown when I went through the waters.

" When thou passest through the waters, I will be with thee; and through the rivers, they shall not overflow thee: when thou walkest through the fire, thou shalt not be burned; neither shall the flame kindle upon thee. **Isaiah 43 :2.**

More proof that God answers prayers, if you will only believe. D'Jean is now twelve years old, is still silently grieving for his mother. He came to see me a week before Thanksgiving in 2019 knowing he can express himself to me. He asked." Have you heard from my Momma at all"? I had not, in over nine months. I placed her name on the prayer request list every week at church and prayed for her every day.

He said it had been a year since he had heard from her. He was keeping time. I told him that she was okay. She was just doing her thing, until God brings her back. I asked," You're worried about your mom aren't you ?"

He answered," Not really, I just hope she's still alive." What a burden for a child to carry. That Sunday he came to church.

When it was time for the altar call he asked me if I was going to the altar. I asked him if he wanted to go, he answered, "Yes." And he led me to the altar. Youth Pastor Derek Stewart asked what his prayer request was. He simply said, "My Mama.'"

Three days later she called and told him she wanted him to spend Thanksgiving with her. Since that day she has been building a relationship with him. After the initial rejoicing for answered prayer, I began to analyze the situation. What is the motive? What is she up to? How long is it going to last? At first I called it a miracle. Then I remembered the promises of God.

"For verily I say unto you, That whosoever shall say unto this mountain, Be thou removed, and be thou cast into the sea; and shall not doubt in his heart, but shall believe that those things which he saith shall come to pass; he shall have whatsoever he saith. Therefore, I say unto you, What things so ever ye desire, when ye pray, believe that ye receive them, and ye shall have them." **Mark 11:23-24 .**

I had asked God for this, and I believed His word. I knew He would do just what He said he would do. So, I am taking him at His word.

After not hearing from my daughter for nine months , we are now rebuilding our relationship daily. She is in a place in her mind that I have not seen her in for years.

God is bringing my Prodigal home, step by step. God has not changed; He will not change . He is the same Yesterday, Today, and Forever. Whatever He has assigned for you to do, do it with all you heart, your soul, and you might.

Whatever you have to suffer, for His sake, ask him for strength, and go through it, He is right there holding your hand.

If you don't know of His saving, healing ,delivering and keeping power, He is available to all that will come to Him.

I know not what my future holds , but I know who holds my future.

I know not what His plan is for me, but I know his plan is perfect.

Vergie Iglus

Vergie Iglus

Author Comments

The purpose of writing this book is not as an expose of any individual who is mentioned in it, but to show how our great God, who is the same yesterday today, and forever. From way back, since the world was formed and man was created, He has never changed. He has brought generations from one dispensation to another. And he has brought man through different seasons of life, and He still does today.

My hopes and my prayers is that everyone who reads it will, not just be entertained by my story but will be inspired. That if you have been facing similar situations such as I have, you can know that there is hope. God is still God. He brought Joseph from the pit to the palace. From the palace to the prison ,and back to the palace again. He is still a mender of broken hearts. and anything else that is broken. He will give you beauty for your ashes, turn your sorrow into joy, if you will only trust Him.

This book is not a book of fiction but about a real life. My life, a vessel that was shattered and broken , but was placed in the hands of the master potter and He made it a brand new vessel. fit for the Masters' use.

Made in the USA
Coppell, TX
26 September 2023

22063756R10154